Greek

LET'S EAT

Greek

Candida Tofallis

Editor
Wendy Hobson

foulsham
LONDON • NEW YORK • TORONTO • SYDNEY

foulsham
Yeovil Road, Slough, Berkshire, SL1 4JH

ISBN 0-572-01800-2

Photoset in Great Britain by Encounter Photosetting, Fleet, Hampshire
Printed in Great Britain by Cox & Wyman Ltd, Reading, Berkshire

Contents

Introduction

If you have enjoyed eating out in a Greek restaurant or adored the food you were served in the tavernas on your Greek holiday, now you can prepare delicious authentic Greek dishes in your own home.

Greeks love their food and enjoy combining the best quality ingredients to produce wonderful dishes. For many of the most famous dishes, however, you will find that different cooks make them in a variety of ways – and each one would insist that their recipe is the best – the only – way of cooking that dish! But you can try as many as you like, experiment with the authentic ingredients and above all enjoy your cooking and your food as the Greeks do.

Many Greek dishes are associated with particular festivals and family occasions. Certainly, in Greece, eating is a social event and friendliness and hospitality are part of the Greek character. You do not have to confine your cooking to yourself or the immediate family. Invite some of your friends to share a meal with you, pour a glass or two of ouzo and enjoy the Greek atmosphere to the full.

Over the past few years, all kinds of more unusual ingredients have become readily available in the supermarkets so it is now quite simple to pick up the ingredients you need to recreate your holiday menu. Any Greek produce which is not readily available has not been included in the recipes.

So go ahead and be adventurous! Try the recipes and enjoy the wonderful flavours of Greek cooking.

Ingredients

Cheeses
Apart from feta cheese, Greek cheeses have not made much of an impact in the supermarkets outside Greece. However, as supermarkets and delicatessens begin to stock more wide-ranging varieties, look out for authentic Greek cheeses for your cooking such as Kaseri, a Cheddar-type cheese and Kefalotyri, a hard grating cheese. Use any strongly flavoured cheeses, such as Cheddar or Gruyère for the recipes.

Chilli Peppers
Chillis give a wonderful spicy touch to Greek cooking, but they do not need to make dishes overhot. Use fresh or dried varieties to suit the recipe and if you do not like the flavour too hot, remove the seeds before you prepare them, as these are the hottest part. After preparation, wash your hands thoroughly as the peppers contain an irritant which will sting your mouth or eyes if you touch them.

Herbs
All the herbs used in these recipes – such as parsley, oregano, rosemary and basil – are available in supermarkets and greengrocers either fresh or dried. Use fresh herbs for the best flavour and texture, and always use fresh herbs for garnishing or sprinkling on cooked dishes.

Mussels
Seafood of all kinds is popular in Greece. Always buy mussels live and fresh and use them on the same day, if possible, or at least the next day, storing them wrapped in newspaper at the bottom of the refrigerator. Preparation details are in the Seafood chapter.

Oil

Many Greek recipes use olive oil, and this is suitable for most dishes. If you prefer, you can use a sunflower oil instead. Virgin olive oil is best for salad dressings as it is of a high quality and has a distinctive flavour.

Olives

Greek cuisine would not be the same without olives. They are available in all sizes and colours and you can experiment until you find the flavours you like best.

Prawns

In Britain, prawns are most often sold peeled and frozen. You can use these prawns for any recipe, but make sure that you do not cook them for too long or they will go rubbery and tasteless. Use a good quality brand. You can also buy uncooked unpeeled prawns. Although these are also usually frozen, they will give a superior flavour. Peel them, if necessary, and remove the black intestinal vein.

Salt Cod

Salt cod is a speciality of Mediterranean countries and is available in Britain in fishmongers or delicatessens. It needs to be desalted before cooking by soaking for at least 24 hours in several changes of fresh water. The soaking time depends on the thickness of the fish, so it is usually easiest to slice the salt cod before soaking so that it can be soaked for the minimum time. After soaking, the fish is drained and usually filleted.

Tomatoes

You can use either fresh or canned tomatoes for most of the recipes in this book. If you use fresh tomatoes, make sure they are ripe and full of flavour. Especially in winter, or if you cannot buy ripe, red tomatoes, you may be better to use the canned varieties.

Equipment

No special equipment is necessary to prepare these dishes in your kitchen. All you really need is a sharp knife, some heavy-based saucepans and frying pans and ovenproof dishes. You may find the following useful but they are not essential.

Barbecue
Food is frequently cooked out of doors in hot countries, so many grilled or roast dishes would traditionally be prepared on a spit over an open charcoal fire. If you have a barbecue you can try out any suitable dishes from this book for a really authentic taste.

Earthenware Casserole
The earthenware casserole is traditional in many Mediterranean countries and varies in size and shape from one region to another. It is a large flameproof dish which can be used on the hob or in the oven, or transferred from one to the other to make cooking – and washing up – easier.

Sieve
Sieving or milling soups, tomatoes or other ingredients can simply be done by rubbing them through an ordinary kitchen sieve, but if you have a food mill or food processor, do use them if you prefer to speed up puréeing or for slicing, chopping and preparing ingredients.

Cooking Methods

Aubergines

Aubergines are a favourite in Greek cookery. They contain bitter juices which need to be drained out before cooking, so they are usually sliced, sprinkled generously with salt and left to drain for about 30 minutes. Rinse them well under running water and pat dry on kitchen paper before continuing with the recipe.

Preparing Chilli Peppers

If you like your food hot and spicy, simply cut off the stem end of the chillis and prepare them with the seeds. The seeds are the strongest part, however, so if you prefer a slightly milder taste – or if you are not sure – discard the seeds and simply chop the flesh.

Always wash your hands after you have prepared chillis as they contain an irritant which will sting if you touch your lips or eyes.

Skinning and Seeding Tomatoes

To skin tomatoes, plunge them into boiling water for about 1 minute then remove with a slotted spoon and place them in a bowl of cold water. You will find that it is then quite easy to cut out the hard stem end of each tomato and slip off the skin. If you want to remove the seeds as well for a really smooth sauce, simply cut each tomato in half and scoop out the seeds with a teaspoon.

Notes on the Recipes

1. Follow one set of measurements only, do not mix metric and Imperial.

2. Eggs are size **2**.

3. Wash fresh produce before preparation.

4. Spoon measurements are level.

5. Adjust seasoning and strongly flavoured ingredients, such as onions and garlic, to suit your own taste.

6. If you substitute dried for fresh herbs, use only half the amount specified.

Appetisers

General Notes

You can serve a selection of Greek appetisers not only to
start a meal, but as cocktail snacks at a party, as light lunch
dishes or on any occasion when a range of tasty and
delicious dishes are required. When calculating quantities,
bear in mind that if you serve a selection of dishes, then
each one will go a little further.

Apart from the recipes included in this section, you can
add other ready-made appetisers to your table. Bowls of
olives, pickled vegetables, sliced sausages, slices of feta
cheese, tomatoes, smoked fish, anchovies are all easy to buy
and can be attractively presented to complement your
selection.

For the perfect combination, serve them with a glass of
chilled ouzo.

1 Taramasalata

Ingredients

175 g/6 oz salted cod roe
45 ml/3 tbsp water
1 onion, finely chopped
2 potatoes, cooked and mashed
250 ml/8 fl oz/1 cup olive oil
Juice of 1 large lemon

Method

1. Blend the fish roe with the water in a blender or food processor. Add the onion and potatoes.

2. Gradually add the oil and lemon juice alternately, blending until the mixture is smooth and light. Chill before serving.

Serves 4

2 Fried Whitebait

Ingredients

1 kg/2 lb whitebait
50 g/2 oz/ 1/2 cup plain flour
Salt and freshly ground black pepper
2.5 ml/ 1/2 tsp cayenne pepper
Olive oil for deep-frying
1 lemon, cut into wedges

Method

1. Wash and clean the fish well. Drain and pat dry on kitchen paper.

2. Place the flour in a plastic bag and season with salt, pepper and cayenne pepper.

3. Add the fish, in batches if necessary, and shake well to coat them evenly. Transfer to a sieve and shake off any excess flour.

4. Heat the oil until very hot. Cook the fish briefly in the hot oil until lightly browned. Drain well on kitchen paper and arrange on a warmed serving plate. Garnish with the lemon wedges and serve with a tomato and onion salad.

Serves 4

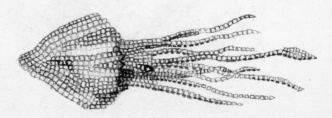

3 Grilled Prawns

Ingredients

30 ml/2 tbsp lemon juice
60 ml/4 tbsp olive oil
1 clove garlic, crushed
5 ml/1 tsp mild mustard
15 ml/1 tbsp chopped fresh parsley
Salt and freshly ground black pepper
1 kg/2 lb large peeled prawns

Method

1. Mix together the lemon juice, oil, garlic, mustard and parsley and season well with salt and pepper.

2. Spread over the prawns and mix well Cover and leave to marinate for at least 1 hour.

3. Cook under a hot grill for about 4 minutes each side. Serve immediately with a green salad.

Serves 4

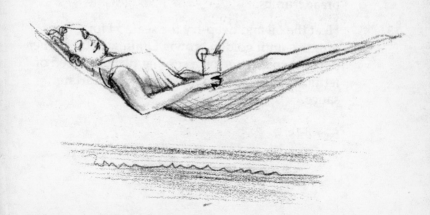

4 | Crispy-Fried Seafood

Ingredients

100 g/4 oz/1 cup plain flour
10 ml/2 tsp salt
2.5 ml/ 1/2 tsp freshly ground white pepper
450 g/1 lb peeled prawns
450 g/1 lb sole fillets, cut into strips
2 egg whites
30 ml/2 tbsp olive oil
100 g/4 oz/1 cup dried breadcrumbs
Oil for deep-frying
Lettuce leaves

Method

1. Mix together the flour, salt and pepper in a plastic bag. Add the prawns and shake until they are well coated. Transfer to a sieve. Add the sole to the bag and shake until well coated. Add to the sieve and shake to remove any excess flour.

2. Whisk the egg whites with the oil. Dip the seafood in the egg white mixture then coat in the breadcrumbs.

3. Heat the oil and deep-fry the seafood for a few minutes until golden brown. Drain well on kitchen paper then arrange on a serving plate on a bed of lettuce leaves. Serve immediately with tartare sauce.

Serves 4

5 Mussels with Wine

Ingredients

100 g/4 oz/ ¹/₂ cup butter or margarine
1 onion, chopped
1 clove garlic, chopped
1 kg/2 lb mussels, scrubbed and bearded
250 ml/8 fl oz/1 cup dry white wine
15 ml/1 tbsp chopped fresh oregano or parsley
Salt and freshly ground black pepper
30 ml/2 tbsp lemon juice

Method

1. Heat the butter or margarine in a large pan and fry the onion and garlic gently for a few minutes until lightly browned.

2. Add the mussels, wine, oregano or parsley and season with salt and pepper. Cover and cook over a high heat for about 5 minutes, shaking the pan occasionally, until all the mussels have opened. Discard any that do not open.

3. Sprinkle with lemon juice, and serve the mussels on warmed deep plates with some of the cooking juices and plenty of fresh bread.

Serves 4

6 Marinated Artichokes

Ingredients

400 g/14 oz canned artichoke hearts, drained
3 cloves garlic, chopped
120 ml/4 fl oz/ ½ cup olive oil
60 ml/4 tbsp white wine vinegar
10 ml/2 tsp oregano
Salt and freshly ground black pepper

Method

1. Place the artichoke hearts in a bowl. Mix together the remaining ingredients and pour over the artichokes. Toss well, cover and chill overnight before serving.

Serves 4

7 Hummus

Ingredients

350 g/12 oz dried chick peas
15 ml/1 tbsp bicarbonate of soda
3 cloves garlic, crushed
Juice of 2 lemons
75 ml/5 tbsp olive oil
100 g/4 oz tahini
Salt and freshly ground black pepper
30 ml/2 tbsp chopped fresh parsley
5 ml/1 tsp paprika

Method

1. Soak the chick peas overnight in cold water with the bicarbonate of soda.

2. Drain and rinse the peas then place them in a saucepan and cover with fresh water. Bring to the boil, skim off any scum, cover and simmer for about 1 1/2 hours until tender. Drain, reserving the cooking liquid.

3. Mash or purée the peas in a food processor. Add the garlic, then add the lemon juice and oil alternately. Beat in the tahini and season with salt and pepper.

4. Turn into a serving bowl and sprinkle with parsley and paprika.

Serves 4

8 Chilli-Cheese Dips

Ingedients

75 ml/5 tbsp olive oil
2 fresh chilli peppers
450 g/1 lb/2 cups feta cheese
15 ml/1 tbsp wine vinegar
Freshly ground black pepper

Method

1. Heat a little of the oil and fry the peppers for a few minutes. Peel them and remove the seeds.

2. Mash the peppers and cheese then gradually work in the remaining oil until the mixture is smooth and soft or process the ingredients in a food processor, adding the oil gradually.

3. Season to taste with wine vinegar and pepper. Serve with crackers.

Serves 4

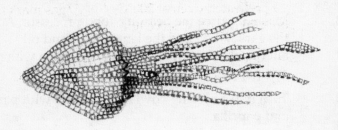

9 Pastry-Wrapped Olives

Ingredients

150 g/5 oz/1¼ cups plain flour
100 g/4 oz/1 cup strong hard cheese, grated
5 ml/1 tsp paprika
120 ml/4 fl oz/ ½ cup corn oil
15 ml/1 tbsp iced water
30 stuffed green olives
60 ml/4 tbsp sesame seeds

Method

1. Mix together the flour, cheese and paprika. Stir in the oil and water and mix to a dough.

2. Wrap small portions of the dough around each olive, rolling in your hands to make small balls.

3. Roll the balls in sesame seeds.

4. Place the balls on a greased baking sheet and bake in a preheated oven at 200°C/400°F/gas mark 6 for about 20 minutes. Serve hot.

Serves 4

10 Bacon-Wrapped Prunes

Ingredients

450 g/1 lb prunes, stoned
50 g/2 oz/ ¹/₂ cup walnut halves
10 rashers streaky bacon, rinded and cut into strips

Method

1. Soak the prunes in water for a few hours. Drain and pat dry.

2. Push a walnut half into the centre of each prune, wrap them in strips of bacon and secure with cocktail sticks. Cover and chill for 1 hour.

3. Arrange on a baking sheet and bake in a preheated oven at 200°C/400°F/gas mark 6 for 15 minutes. Serve at once.

Serves 4

11 | Stuffed Mushrooms

Ingredients

225 g/8 oz large mushrooms
Salt
5 ml/1 tsp lemon juice
15 ml/1 tbsp olive oil
15 ml/1 tbsp butter or margarine
1 onion, finely chopped
30 ml/2 tbsp dry white wine
Freshly ground black pepper
30 ml/2 tbsp double cream
100 g/4 oz/1 cup Gruyère cheese, grated
15 ml/1 tbsp chopped fresh parsley
25 g/1 oz/ 1/4 cup Parmesan cheese, grated

Method

1. Blanch the mushrooms in boiling salted water with the lemon juice for 30 seconds. Drain well. Remove and chop the mushroom stems.

2. Heat the oil and butter or margarine and fry the onion for a few minutes until soft. Add the mushroom stems and wine and season with salt and pepper. Simmer until the liquid has evaporated.

3. Remove from the heat and stir in the cream, cheese and parsley.

4. Use the mixture to stuff the mushroom caps then sprinkle with Parmesan. Grill them under a preheated grill for about 10 minutes until browned and bubbling. Serve at once.

Serves 4

12 Fried Courgettes and Aubergine

Ingredients

450 g/1 lb aubergines, sliced
450 g/1 lb courgettes, sliced
Salt
5 ml/1 tsp dried yeast
250 ml/8 fl oz/1 cup warm water
225 g/8 oz/2 cups plain flour
Oil for deep-frying

Method

1. Arrange the aubergines and courgettes in two colanders and sprinkle generously with salt. Leave to stand for 1 hour. Rinse and drain.

2. Dissolve the yeast in a little warm water. Beat in the flour and remaining water and continue to beat until the mixture forms a smooth batter.

3. Heat the oil. Dip the courgettes and aubergines in the batter and fry in the hot oil, a few at a time, until golden brown. Drain on kitchen paper and serve with Tzatziki (page 27).

Serves 4

13 Tzatziki

Ingredients

750 ml/1 ¹/₄ pts/3 cups Greek yoghurt
1 cucumber, peeled and chopped
4 cloves garlic, crushed
45 ml/3 tbsp olive oil
Salt
45 ml/3 tbsp chopped fresh dill

Method

1. Line a sieve with muslin or double-thick kitchen paper and place the yoghurt in it. Leave to drain for about 2 hours.

2. Transfer the yoghurt to a bowl and stir in the cucumber, garlic and oil. Season with salt, cover and chill.

3. Serve sprinkled with dill.

Serves 4-6

14	Stuffed Vine Leaves

Ingredients

225 g/8 oz preserved vine leaves
6 spring onions, chopped
1 onion, chopped
225 g/8 oz/1 cup medium-grain rice
45 ml/3 tbsp chopped fresh parsley
250 ml/8 fl oz/1 cup olive oil
Salt and freshly ground black pepper
300 ml/1/2 pt/1 1/4 cups boiling water
45 ml/3 tbsp lemon juice

Method

1. Blanch the vine leaves in boiling water. Drain and leave to cool.

2. Place the onions in a sieve and sprinkle with salt. Rinse with water and squeeze out excess moisture.

3. Mix the onions with the rice, parsley and half the oil and season with salt and pepper.

4. Reserve a few vine leaves. Place a spoonful of the mixture on each of the remaining leaves, fold over the sides and roll into neat parcels.

5. Arrange the reserved leaves on the base of a flameproof casserole and top with the stuffed vine leaves. Pour over the remaining oil, water and lemon juice. Place a heavy plate on top, cover and bring to the boil. Reduce the heat and simmer for about 40 minutes until all the liquid has been absorbed.

6. Leave to cool in the pan then transfer to a serving plate and serve with Tzatziki (page 27) or yoghurt.

Serves 4

15 Fried Broad Beans

Ingredients

450 g/1 lb broad beans
Salt
50 g/2 oz/ 1/2 cup plain flour
Freshly ground black pepper
A pinch of cayenne pepper
60 ml/4 tbsp olive oil
175 ml/6 fl oz/ 3/4 cup mayonnaise
45 ml/3 tbsp tomato purée

Method

1. Blanch the beans in boiling salted water for 2 minutes then drain well.

2. Season the flour with salt, pepper and cayenne pepper and toss the beans in the flour.

3. Heat the oil and fry the beans, stirring continuously, for about 5 minutes until just tender and lightly browned. Remove from the pan and drain on kitchen paper.

4. Mix together the mayonnaise and tomato purée to taste and season with salt and pepper. Serve as a dip with the beans.

Serves 4

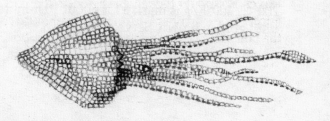

16 Pastrami-Pastry Rolls

Ingredients

10 slices pastrami
2 eggs, beaten
250 ml/8 fl oz/1 cup olive oil
4 spring onions, chopped
1 packet filo pastry
10 slices Gruyère cheese
100 g/4 oz/1 cup strong hard cheese, grated
50 g/2 oz/¼ cup sesame seeds

Method

1. Soak the pastrami in the eggs for at least 1 hour.

2. Heat 45 ml/3 tbsp of oil and fry the spring onions for a few minutes until soft. Remove from the heat.

3. Warm the remaining oil and brush it over half of each filo pastry sheet then fold the sheets in half. Place a slice of Gruyère cheese near one end of each pastry sheet. Place a slice of pastrami on top and sprinkle with onion and grated cheese. Fold the pastry over the filling, brush with oil then roll up.

4. Place the rolls on a greased baking sheet and brush with oil and the remaining eggs. Sprinkle with sesame seeds and bake in a preheated oven at 200°C/400°F/gas mark 6 for about 10 minutes until golden brown. Serve at once.

Serves 4

17 Eggs with Pepper Sauce

Ingredients

8 eggs, beaten
100 g/4 oz feta cheese, crumbled
15 ml/1 tbsp chopped fresh parsley
120 ml/4 fl oz/¹/₂ cup Red Pepper Sauce (page 152)
25 g/1 oz/2 tbsp butter or margarine
Salt and freshly ground black pepper

Method

1. Beat the eggs and mix in the cheese, parsley and pepper sauce.

2. Heat the butter or margarine and fry the egg mixture, stirring occasionally, until cooked through. Season with salt and pepper and serve at once.

Serves 4

18 Anchovy-Stuffed Eggs

Ingredients

4 hard-boiled eggs
50 g/2 oz anchovies, drained
45 ml/3 tbsp mayonnaise
10 ml/2 tsp lemon juice
Salt and freshly ground black pepper
10 ml/2 tsp chopped fresh parsley

Method

1. Halve the eggs lengthways and scoop out the yolks. Mash 2 of the anchovies and mix them with the egg yolks, mayonnaise and lemon juice. Season with salt and pepper.

2. Spoon or pipe the mixture back into the egg whites and sprinkle with parsley.

3. Twist the remaining anchovies into rolls and use to garnish the eggs.

Serves 4

19 | Cheese Squares

Ingredients

25 g/1 oz/¹/4 cup plain flour
Salt and freshly ground black pepper
225 g/8 oz strong hard cheese, cubed
120 ml/4 fl oz/¹/2 cup olive oil
Juice of 1 lemon

Method

1. Season the flour with salt and pepper. Roll the cheese cubes in the flour to coat them thoroughly.

2. Heat the oil until smoking then fry the cheese cubes briefly, turning once, until crisp and brown. Transfer to a warmed serving plate, sprinkle with lemon juice and serve at once.

Serves 4

Soups

A hearty, warming soup is a staple meal in many a Greek household during the winter months, rich with meat, chicken, pulses and vegetables and thickened with mashed potatoes or vegetables. Think of Greek soups not just as an introduction to a meal, but as a meal in themselves, served with plenty of crusty bread and perhaps a tasty salad.

Chick Pea Soup

Ingredients

675 g/1 1/2 lb dried chick peas
15 ml/1 tbsp bicarbonate of soda
3 onions, chopped
175 ml/6 fl oz/3/4 cup olive oil
Salt and freshly ground black pepper
Juice of 1 lemon
30 ml/2 tbsp chopped fresh parsley

Method

1. Soak the chick peas overnight in cold water with the bicarbonate of soda.

2. Drain the chick peas well and place them in a large saucepan. Cover with fresh water, bring to the boil and skim off any scum. Add the onions, cover and simmer gently for about 1 1/2 hours until the peas are tender, adding a little more cold water from time to time to keep the peas covered.

3. Add the oil and season with salt and pepper. Remove the lid and continue to simmer for about 10 minutes or until ready to serve.

4. Stir in the lemon juice and sprinkle with parsley before serving.

Serves 4

2 Lentil Soup

Ingredients

> 250 ml/8 fl oz/1 cup olive oil
> 2 onions, chopped
> 4 cloves garlic, crushed
> 400 g/14 oz canned tomatoes, drained and sieved
> 450 g/1 lb lentils
> 30 ml/2 tbsp white wine vinegar
> 5 ml/1 tsp sugar
> 1 bay leaf
> 5 ml/1 tsp chopped fresh parsley
> Salt and freshly ground black pepper

Method

1. Heat the oil in a large pan and fry the onions and garlic gently for 5 minutes until just soft, without allowing them to brown.

2. Add the tomatoes and bring to the boil. Add the lentils and stir in the wine vinegar, sugar, bay leaf and parsley and season with salt and pepper.

3. Bring back to the boil, cover and simmer gently for about 1 hour until the lentils are tender, topping up with a little boiling water or stock if the soup is not of the desired consistency. Season with pepper before serving.

Serves 4

3 | Tomato Soup

Ingredients

750 ml/1 ¼ pts/3 cups chicken or vegetable stock
400 g/14 oz canned tomatoes, drained and sieved
30 ml/2 tbsp olive oil
100 g/4 oz soup pasta
30 ml/2 tbsp chopped fresh parsley
Salt and freshly ground black pepper

Method

1. Place the stock, tomatoes and oil in a large saucepan, bring to the boil, cover and simmer for about 30 minutes, stirring occasionally.

2. Add the pasta and simmer for a further 15 minutes until the pasta is tender. If the soup is not the consistency you prefer, thin down with a little water or stock, or remove the lid and boil until reduced and thickened slightly.

3. Stir in the parsley and season well with salt and pepper before serving.

Serves 4

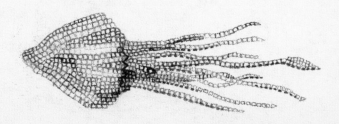

4 Vegetable Broth

Ingredients

1 onion, sliced
1 carrot, sliced
1 leek, sliced
1 stick celery, sliced
1 clove garlic, crushed
1 green pepper, chopped
1.5 l/2 ½ pts/6 cups water
4 sprigs parsley
5 ml/1 tsp peppercorns
5 ml/1 tsp salt

Method

1. Place all the ingredients in a large saucepan, bring to the boil, cover and simmer for about 30 minutes.

2. Strain and use as the base for another soup or as a broth with dumplings.

Serves 4

5 | Cauliflower Soup

Ingredients

60 ml/4 tbsp olive oil
3 onions, chopped
1 clove garlic, crushed
2 potatoes, chopped
1/2 cauliflower, cut into small florets
400 g/14 oz canned tomatoes, chopped
175 g/6 oz soup pasta
30 ml/2 tbsp chopped fresh parsley
Salt and freshly ground black pepper
1 egg, beaten
50 g/2 oz/1/2 cup Parmesan cheese, grated

Method

1. Heat the oil in a heavy-based saucepan and fry the onions and garlic for about 4 minutes until just soft.

2. Add the potatoes and cauliflower and fry for 2 minutes.

3. Add the tomatoes and just cover the ingredients with water. Bring to the boil, cover and simmer for about 10 minutes until the vegetables are tender.

4. Stir in the pasta and parsley and season with salt and pepper. Continue to simmer for about 10 minutes until the pasta is cooked.

5. Stir in the egg and sprinkle with Parmesan before serving.

Serves 4

6 Egg and Lemon Soup

Ingredients

2 l/3 1/2 pts/8 1/2 cups chicken stock
50 g/2 oz/ 1/4 cup long-grain rice
Juice of 1 lemon
2 egg yolks, beaten
Salt and freshly ground black pepper

Method

1. Bring the stock to the boil, add the rice and simmer gently for about 20 minutes until the rice is tender. Remove from the heat.

2. Beat the lemon juice into the egg yolks and season well with salt and pepper.

3. Beat 250 ml/8 fl oz/1 cup of warm stock into the egg mixture. Return the stock to a low heat and pour the egg mixture into the saucepan. Heat through gently before serving.

Serves 4

7 Fish Soup

Ingredients

2 onions, chopped
1 carrot, chopped
2 sticks celery, chopped
1 bay leaf
2 sprigs parsley
1.75 l/3 pts/7 1/2 cups water
120 ml/4 fl oz/ 1/2 cup olive oil
Salt and freshly ground black pepper
1 kg/2 lb fish, cleaned, scaled and cut into chunks
1 quantity Oil and Lemon Dressing (page 131)
30 ml/2 tbsp chopped fresh parsley
1 quantity Egg and Lemon Sauce (page 148)

Method

1. Place the vegetables, bay leaf, parsley, water and olive oil in a heavy-based saucepan and season with salt and pepper. Bring to the boil, cover and simmer for about 30 minutes until the vegetables are tender.

2. Place the fish in a frying basket or strainer and lower it into the stock, return to the boil, cover and simmer for a further 15 minutes until the fish is cooked.

3. Transfer the fish to a warmed serving dish, spoon over a little oil and lemon dressing and garnish with the parsley. Strain the stock into a clean saucepan and heat through gently. Stir in the egg and lemon sauce and serve with the fish with the remaining oil and lemon dressing served separately.

Serves 4.

8 Semolina Soup with Meatballs

Ingredients

450 g/1 lb minced beef
2 onions, finely chopped
2 cloves garlic, crushed
15 ml/1 tbsp chopped fresh parsley
50 g/2 oz/ 1/3 cup cooked long-grain rice
Salt and freshly ground black pepper
1 egg, beaten
1.2 l/2 pts/5 cups chicken or vegetable stock
1 large tomato, skinned and chopped
15 ml/1 tbsp olive oil
2 egg yolks
Juice of 1 lemon
10 ml/2 tsp semolina

Method

1. Mix together the beef, 1 onion, the garlic, parsley and rice and season with salt and pepper. Bind the mixture with the egg and shape into small balls.

2. Bring the stock to the boil with the remaining onion, the tomato and oil. Add the meatballs and simmer for about 35 minutes until the meat is tender. Remove from the heat and leave to cool slightly.

3. Beat the egg yolks and lemon juice. Pour in 250 ml/8 fl oz/1 cup of stock and mix in the semolina.

4. Return the semolina mixture to the pan and reheat gently without allowing the mixture to boil, stirring until the soup thickens.

Serves 4

Seafood

General Notes

In a country with such a tradition of fishing, naturally
Greece boasts a huge range of fish recipes, ranging from the
everyday to the exotic. Providing nutritious and tasty
meals, fish can be cooked in a fraction of the time of many
other main ingredients, making it convenient for the
modern busy cook.

Fish is very versatile. It can be grilled, baked, steamed or
fried, and you can substitute any similar fish to the one
mentioned in the recipe to suit the freshest and best
ingredients available to you.

Try to buy fish as fresh as possible. It should be shiny
with bright eyes and have a fresh smell. If not, leave it
alone. Clean and wash the fish straight away, wrap it well
and store it in the refrigerator until you are ready to cook. It
should not be kept for more than a day. Shellfish, in
particular, must be very fresh and should be cooked and
eaten on the day of purchase, if possible. Many shellfish,
such as mussels, should be bought alive. It is often worth
buying slightly more than you need, as you will have to

discard a few during preparation and cooking. Crab and lobster are also available live, although in Britain most people prefer to buy them already cooked. Most prawns in Britain are sold already cooked and often frozen. Do try to buy them fresh, if possible, or choose a good quality frozen variety. You can buy uncooked frozen prawns in many fishmongers and some supermarkets and these are worth trying as they have a far superior flavour.

Some fish are cooked whole, in which case they need to be gutted and sometimes scaled. Slit the fish down the belly and gently scrape out all the innards. You can leave on the head, in which case make sure you remove the gills, or you can cut it off. Scale a fish in the sink as it is a messy job. Hold the fish by the tail, using a piece of cloth or kitchen paper to help you grasp it firmly, if necessary. Using the flat blade of a knife, scrape away from you to take off the scales. Wash the fish thoroughly.

Shellfish such as mussels should be soaked in several changes of fresh water for a few hours so that they can open up to filter out any sand or grit. If any of them do not open, throw them away – they are not fresh. Scrub the shellfish thoroughly, and remove the weed-like beards from mussels with a sharp knife. Leave them soaking in cold water until you are ready to cook them. If any do not open while cooking, discard them; never try to force them open.

If you can use uncooked prawns for the recipes, you will obtain the tastiest results. To peel them, remove the outer shell and take out the grey intestinal vein which runs down the back. If you use cooked prawns, they only need the minimum amount of cooking. Shellfish which is overcooked will lose its flavour and have a rubbery texture.

1 Baked Haddock with Garlic

Ingredients

5 cloves garlic, crushed
5 ml/1 tsp oregano
30 ml/2 tbsp chopped fresh parsley
Juice of 1/2 lemon
Salt and freshly ground black pepper
175 g/12 oz haddock
30 ml/2 tbsp olive oil

Method

1. Mix together the garlic, oregano, parsley and lemon juice and season with salt and pepper. Rub the mixture over the inside and outside of the fish and lay it on a large sheet of kitchen foil.

2. Pour the oil over the fish and seal the top of the foil. Bake in a preheated oven at 180°C/350°F/gas mark 4 for about 30 minutes until the fish is tender. Serve with a potato salad.

Serves 4

2 Fish Croquettes

Ingredients

1 kg/2 lb dried salt cod
50 g/2 oz/1/4 cup butter or margarine
50 g/2 oz/1/2 cup plain flour
375 ml/13 fl oz/1 1/2 cups milk
Salt and freshly ground black pepper
A pinch of nutmeg
4 eggs, lightly beaten
30 ml/2 tbsp chopped fresh parsley
Flour for coating
15 ml/1 tbsp olive oil
100 g/4 oz/1 cup dried breadcrumbs
Oil for deep-frying

Method

1. Remove the skin from the fish and cut into large chunks. Soak in cold water for 24 hours, changing the water several times. Drain well, remove the bones and flake the fish.

2. Melt the butter or margarine, stir in the flour and cook for 1 minute without letting the flour brown. Stir in the milk, bring to the boil, stirring, and simmer until the sauce thickens. Remove from the heat and leave to cool slightly.

3. Fold 2 eggs into the sauce then stir in the fish and season with salt, pepper and nutmeg. Cool, cover and refrigerate for several hours.

4. Shape the mixture into small balls and roll in flour. Beat the remaining eggs with the olive oil. Dip the croquettes into the egg mixture then roll in the breadcrumbs until well coated.

5.   Heat the oil and deep-fry the croquettes until golden brown. Drain well and serve with salad.

Serves 4-6

DOLMADES

3 Baked Sardines

Ingredients

1 kg/2 lb sardines
Salt and freshly ground black pepper
Juice of 1 lemon
30 ml/2 tbsp olive oil
2 onions, sliced
2 cloves garlic, crushed
200 g/7 oz canned tomatoes
120 ml/4 fl oz/1/2 cup dry white wine
30 ml/2 tbsp chopped fresh dill
90 ml/6 tbsp water
30 ml/2 tbsp chopped fresh parsley

Method

1. Prepare the fish and lay them in an oiled roasting tin. Sprinkle with salt, pepper and lemon juice.

2. Heat the oil in a frying pan and fry the onions and garlic for 5 minutes until soft. Add the tomatoes, wine, dill and water, cover and simmer for 25 minutes, stirring occasionally.

3. Pour the sauce over the fish and bake in a preheated oven at 180°C/350°F/gas mark 4 for 30 minutes until the fish is tender. Sprinkle with parsley and serve hot or cold.

Serves 4

4 Red Snapper with Olives

Ingredients

2 red snapper
Salt and freshly ground black pepper
250 ml/8 fl oz/1 cup olive oil
2 onions, thinly sliced
4 cloves garlic, sliced
1 red pepper, cut into strips
3 tomatoes, skinned, deseeded and chopped
250 ml/8 fl oz/1 cup dry white wine
30 ml/2 tbsp chopped fresh parsley
100 g/4 oz black olives, stoned

Method

1. Clean, scale and wash the fish. Drain well. Make a few diagonal cuts on each side of the fish and season with salt and pepper.

2. Heat the oil and fry the onions, garlic and pepper for about 5 minutes until soft but not browned. Add the tomatoes and simmer for about 10 minutes until thickened.

3. Add the wine and parsley and season with salt and pepper. Simmer for 4 minutes.

4. Arrange half the mixture on the base of a greased ovenproof dish, lay the fish on top and cover with the remaining mixture. Scatter with the olives.

5. Cover and bake in a preheated oven at 190°C/375°F/gas mark 5 for about 1 hour until the fish is tender.

Serves 4

5 Shark Steaks in Lemon Juice

Ingredients

4 shark steaks
Salt and freshly ground black pepper
30 ml/2 tbsp plain flour
120 ml/4 fl oz/¹/₂ cup olive oil
Juice of 1 lemon
1 clove garlic, crushed
5 ml/1 tsp oregano
2 sprigs parsley

Method

1. Season the steaks with salt and pepper and dust with flour. Heat the oil, lemon juice, garlic and oregano and fry the steaks until cooked through and lightly browned on both sides.

2. Transfer to a warmed serving plate and garnish with the parsley. Serve with tartare sauce.

Serves 4

6 Fried Salt Cod

Ingredients

675 g/1 ¹/₂ lb salt cod
3 eggs
45 ml/3 tbsp water
100 g/4 oz/1 cup plain flour
Salt and freshly ground black pepper
Oil for frying
1 lemon, sliced
4 fresh parsley sprigs

Method

1. Skin the salt cod and cut it into thick slices. Soak it in several changes of water for at least 24 hours. Drain well.

2. Beat the eggs and water then beat in the flour to make a smooth thick batter. Season with salt and pepper.

3. Heat 1 cm/ ¹/₂ in of oil in a frying pan. Dip the fish into the batter and fry in the hot oil for about 10 minutes until crisp and golden on both sides. Drain on kitchen paper then arrange on a warmed serving plate and serve garnished with the lemon slices and parsley.

Serves 4

7 Steamed Wine Prawns

Ingredients

900 g/2 lb uncooked prawns
150 ml/ 1/4 pt/ 2/3 cup dry white wine
Salt and freshly ground black pepper
150 ml/ 1/4 pt/ 2/3 cup Oil and Lemon Dressing (page 131)
30 ml/2 tbsp chopped fresh parsley

Method

1. Peel and devein the prawns, leaving on the heads and tails if possible.

2. Season the wine with salt and pepper and bring to the boil in the bottom half of a steamer. Place the prawns on top in a steamer rack and simmer for about 8 minutes, shaking the pan occasionally, until the prawns have turned pink. If you use cooked prawns, halve the cooking time.

3. Transfer the prawns to a serving plate and dress with the oil and lemon dressing. Sprinkle with parsley and serve warm or cold.

Serves 4

8 | Avocado Prawns

Ingredients

2 avocados
30 ml/2 tbsp lemon juice
Salt
150 ml/ ¼ pt/ ⅔ cup mayonnaise
Freshly ground black pepper
450 g/1 lb cooked peeled prawns
15 ml/1 tbsp chopped fresh parsley
½ bunch of watercress

Method

1. Slice the avocados in half lengthways, remove the stones and brush with lemon juice. Season with salt.

2. Season the mayonnaise with salt and pepper. Arrange a few prawns in the hollow of each avocado and spoon over the mayonnaise. Arrange the remaining prawns on top and sprinkle with parsley. Serve garnished with watercress.

Serves 4

9 Prawn Kebabs

Ingredients

675 g/1 1/2 lb large prawns
8 rashers bacon, rinded and cut into strips
1 green pepper, cut into chunks
Salt and freshly ground black pepper
150 ml/1/4 pt/2/3 cup olive oil
150 ml/1/4 pt/2/3 cup mayonnaise
2.5 ml/1/2 tsp cayenne pepper
1/2 lettuce, shredded

Method

1. Peel and devein the prawns, if necessary, leaving the tails intact.

2. Wrap each prawn in a strip of bacon and thread on to skewers, alternating with chunks of pepper. Season with salt and pepper and brush well with oil.

3. Grill the kebabs under a preheated grill for about 10 minutes, turning and brushing frequently with more oil.

4. Season the mayonnaise with cayenne pepper, salt and pepper.

5. Serve the kebabs on a bed of lettuce with the mayonnaise served separately.

Serves 4

10 | Prawns with Feta Cheese

Ingredients

120 ml/4 fl oz/¹/₂ cup olive oil
2 onions, chopped
2 cloves garlic, crushed
400 g/14 oz canned tomatoes, chopped
30 ml/2 tbsp tomato purée
250 ml/8 fl oz/1 cup dry white wine
45 ml/3 tbsp chopped fresh parsley
5 ml/1 tsp oregano
Salt and freshly ground black pepper
100 g/4 oz feta cheese, crumbled
450 g/1 lb cooked peeled prawns

Method

1. Heat the oil and fry the onions and garlic for about 5 minutes until soft. Add the tomatoes, tomato purée, wine, parsley and oregano and season with salt and pepper. Bring to the boil, partially cover and simmer gently for about 30 minutes, stirring occasionally, until the sauce has thickened.

2. Add the cheese and prawns and simmer gently for about 5 minutes, stirring, until heated through. Serve with crusty bread.

Serves 4

11 Fried Squid Rings

Ingredients

900 g/2 lb small squid
Salt
50 g/2 oz/1/2 cup plain flour
Oil for deep frying
Juice of 2 lemons

Method

1. To prepare the squid, remove the skin and pull the body and tentacles apart. Remove and discard the plastic-like quill and cut off the eyes and beak. The body and tentacles are edible. Clean thoroughly and slice into rings.

2. Sprinkle the squid with salt and coat lightly with flour.

3. Heat the oil and fry the squid rings for a few minutes until lightly browned. Drain well on kitchen paper then arrange on a warmed serving plate and sprinkle with lemon juice. Serve with Garlic and Potato Sauce (page 149).

Serves 4

12 Squid in Tomato Sauce

Ingredients

1 kg/2 lb squid or cuttlefish
250 ml/8 fl oz/1 cup olive oil
2 onions, chopped
2 cloves garlic, chopped
250 ml/8 fl oz/1 cup dry white wine
400 g/14 oz canned tomatoes
30 ml/2 tbsp chopped fresh parsley
Salt and freshly ground black pepper

Method

1. To prepare the squid or cuttlefish, remove the skin and pull the body from the tentacles. Remove and discard the plastic-like quill and cut off the eyes and beak. Cut the body and tentacles into strips.

2. Heat the oil and fry the onions and garlic for about 5 minutes until soft. Add the squid and fry until lightly browned.

3. Add the wine, tomatoes and parsley and season with salt and pepper. Bring to the boil, cover and simmer over a low heat for about 1 hour until the squid is tender, adding a little water during cooking, if necessary. Serve with rice or noodles.

Serves 4

Poultry and Game

There are a number of delicious chicken dishes cooked in Greece, and the Greeks are also fond of small game birds which are now readily available in British supermarkets.

1 Chicken Rissoles

Ingredients

450 g/1 lb chicken meat, minced
1 onion, finely chopped
1 potato, grated
50 g/2 oz/1/2 cup dried breadcrumbs
30 ml/2 tbsp chopped fresh parsley
5 ml/1 tsp oregano
Salt and freshly ground black pepper
2 eggs, beaten
Oil for frying

Method

1. Mix together the chicken, onion, potato, 45 ml/3 tbsp of breadcrumbs, the parsley and oregano and season with salt and pepper. Bind the mixture with the eggs, shape into balls and flatten them slightly.

2. Coat the rissoles in the remaining breadcrumbs.

3. Heat the oil and fry the rissoles for about 15 minutes until cooked through and golden brown on both sides.

Serves 4

2 Chicken with Okra

Ingredients

30 ml/2 tbsp olive oil
4 chicken portions
2 onions, chopped
3 cloves garlic, chopped
120 ml/4 fl oz/¹/₂ cup dry red wine
400 g/14 oz canned tomatoes, chopped
30 ml/2 tbsp tomato purée
1 bay leaf
30 ml/2 tbsp chopped fresh parsley
1 stick cinnamon
120 ml/4 fl oz/¹/₂ cup water
Salt and freshly ground black pepper
225 g/8 oz okra, sliced

Method

1. Heat the oil and fry the chicken portions until lightly browned on all sides. Remove from the pan.

2. Add the onions and garlic and fry for about 5 minutes until soft. Add the wine and simmer for 1 minute. Add the tomatoes, tomato purée, bay leaf, parsley, cinnamon and water and season with salt and pepper. Bring to the boil, cover and simmer gently for about 30 minutes until the chicken is cooked, adding a little more water during cooking, if necessary.

3. Add the okra, cover and simmer for a further 10 minutes until the okra is tender. Discard the bay leaf and cinnamon. Serve hot with rice.

Serves 4

3 Filo Chicken Pie with Cream Sauce

Ingredients

75 ml/5 tbsp olive oil
2 onions, chopped
1 clove garlic, crushed
2 rashers bacon, rinded and chopped
450 g/1 lb cooked chicken, chopped
15 ml/1 tbsp chopped fresh parsley
A pinch of grated nutmeg
Salt and freshly ground black pepper
10 sheets filo pastry
15 ml/1 tbsp sesame seeds

For the sauce:
30 ml/2 tbsp butter or margarine
30 ml/2 tbsp plain flour
300 ml/1/2 pt/1 1/4 cups milk
50 g/2 oz/1/2 cup Parmesan cheese, grated
1 egg, beaten

Method

1. Heat 30 ml/2 tbsp of olive oil and fry the onions and garlic for about 5 minutes until soft. Add the bacon and fry for a further 3 minutes. Remove from the heat and stir in the chicken, parsley and nutmeg and season with salt and pepper.

2. Brush half the filo pastry with some of the remaining oil and arrange in the base of a greased pie dish. Spoon in the chicken mixture. Brush the remaining sheets with oil and cover the pie. Seal the edges and sprinkle the top with water then sesame seeds.

3.   Bake in a preheated oven at 190°C/375°F/gas
     mark 5 for 30 minutes until golden brown.

4.   Meanwhile, melt the butter or margarine, stir in
     the flour and cook gently for 1 minute. Stir in
     the milk and bring to the boil, stirring
     continuously. Simmer, stirring, until the sauce
     thickens. Remove from the heat and stir in the
     cheese and egg. Season with salt and pepper and
     serve with the pie.

Serves 4

4 Red Chicken

Ingredients

30 ml/2 tbsp olive oil
4 chicken portions
1 onion, chopped
1 clove garlic, crushed
2 sticks celery, chopped
250 ml/8 fl oz/1 cup dry red wine
400 g/14 oz canned tomatoes, chopped
15 ml/1 tbsp tomato purée
30 ml/2 tbsp chopped fresh parsley
Salt and freshly ground black pepper

Method

1.   Heat the oil in a heavy-based saucepan and fry the chicken portions until golden brown and sealed on all sides. Remove from the pan.

2.   Add the onion, garlic and celery to the pan and fry for about 4 minutes until just soft. Add the wine and simmer for 1 minute.

3.   Return the chicken to the pan. Add the tomatoes, tomato purée and parsley and season with salt and pepper. Bring to the boil, cover and simmer for about 40 minutes until the chicken is cooked through and the sauce has thickened.

4.   Add a little water during cooking, if necessary, if the sauce is too thick. If the sauce is too thin, remove the lid for the last portion of the cooking time.

Serves 4

5 Chicken with Orange Juice

Ingredients

1 chicken
Salt and freshly ground black pepper
3 cloves garlic, crushed
5 ml/1 tsp oregano
Juice of 1 lemon
300 ml/ 1/2 pt/1 1/4 cups water
50 g/2 oz/ 1/4 cup butter or margarine
Juice of 2 oranges

Method

1. Season the chicken inside and out with salt and pepper and place it in a deep baking dish. Add the garlic, oregano, lemon juice and water to the dish. Dot the chicken with the butter or margarine. Bake the chicken in a preheated oven at 200°C/400°F/ gas mark 6 for 30 minutes, basting occasionally.

2. Turn the chicken over and pour half the orange juice over the chicken. Return to the oven for 30 minutes, basting frequently.

3. Turn the chicken again and pour over the remaining orange juice. Return to the oven for a further 30 minutes or until cooked through, basting frequently.

Serves 4

Chicken with Lemon Sauce

Ingredients

1 chicken
2 cloves
2 onions
2 sticks celery, sliced
2 carrots, sliced
30 ml/2 tbsp plain flour
1 egg yolk
Juice of 1 lemon
Salt and freshly ground black pepper

Method

1. Place the chicken in a heavy-based saucepan. Stud a clove into each onion and add them to the pan with the celery and carrots. Fill the pan with water to half way up the legs of the chicken. Bring to the boil, cover and simmer for about 1 hour until the chicken is tender.

2. Remove the chicken from the pan. Skin and debone the chicken and cut into large pieces. Strain the stock into a clean pan. Mix the flour with a little stock and stir it into pan. Bring to the boil, stirring until the sauce thickens. Remove from the heat and leave to cool slightly.

3. Beat together the egg yolk and lemon juice and stir it into the stock. Return the chicken to the pan and heat very gently, stirring continuously, until the sauce thickens. Serve with rice.

Serves 4

7 Quails with Bacon

Ingredients

4 quails
Salt and freshly ground black pepper
120 ml/4 fl oz/ 1/2 cup olive oil
5 ml/1 tsp dried oregano
4 bacon rashers, rinded
450 g/1 lb large mushrooms
4 onions, sliced
2 green peppers, sliced

Method

1. Sprinkle the quails inside and out with salt and pepper, brush with oil and sprinkle with a little oregano. Wrap each one in a bacon rasher and arrange on skewers, alternating with mushrooms. Arrange the remaining mushrooms on separate skewers. Brush again with oil and sprinkle with salt, pepper and oregano.

2. Grill the quails and mushrooms under a moderate grill for about 30 minutes, turning frequently and basting with the meat juices and a little more oil if necessary, until the birds are cooked and the bacon and skins are crispy.

3. Meanwhile, heat the remaining oil in a frying pan and fry the onions and peppers for about 8 minutes until soft and lightly browned. Season with salt and pepper.

4. Arrange the onions and peppers in the base of a warmed shallow serving dish and top with the quails and mushrooms.

Serves 4

8 Pheasant with Orange and Nuts

Ingredients

60 ml/4 tbsp olive oil
50 g/2 oz/1/2 cup almonds
50 g/2 oz/1/2 cup pine kernels
50 g/2 oz/1/2 cup plain flour
Salt and freshly ground black pepper
1 pheasant, cut into portions
150 ml/1/4 pt/2/3 cup dry white wine
90 ml/6 tbsp orange juice
15 ml/1 tbsp lemon juice
1 orange, sliced
15 ml/1 tbsp chopped fresh parsley

Method

1. Heat the oil and fry the almonds and pine kernels for a few minutes until lightly browned. Remove from the pan and put to one side.

2. Season the flour with salt and pepper and use to coat the pheasant portions. Fry the pheasant in the oil until lightly browned on all sides.

3. Add the wine, bring to the boil, cover and simmer gently for about 40 minutes until the pheasant is tender.

4. Transfer the pheasant to a warmed serving plate and keep it warm. Add the nuts, orange juice and lemon juice to the sauce, bring to the boil and boil until reduced to the consistency you prefer. Season with salt and pepper and pour over the pheasant. Serve garnished with the orange slices and a little chopped parsley.

Serves 4

Meat

Lamb is particularly popular in Greece and there are many delicious recipes. Grilled and fried meats are often served with a selection of salads and crusty breads.

1 Spicy Lamb Stew

Ingredients

30 ml/2 tbsp plain flour
Salt and freshly ground black pepper
1 kg/2 lb lean lamb, cubed
90 ml/6 tbsp olive oil
2 onions, chopped
2 cloves garlic, crushed
1 red chilli pepper, chopped
400 g/14 oz canned tomatoes
15 ml/1 tbsp tomato purée
30 ml/2 tbsp dry white wine
1 stick cinnamon
3 cloves
350 g/12 oz macaroni
1 sprig of parsley

Method

1. Season the flour with salt and pepper and toss the lamb in the flour until well coated. Shake off any excess.

2. Heat the oil and fry the meat until browned on all sides. Remove from the pan with a slotted spoon.

3. Add the onions, garlic and chilli pepper to the pan and fry for about 5 minutes until soft. Add the tomatoes, tomato purée, wine, cinnamon and cloves and bring to the boil. Season with salt and pepper.

4. Return the meat to the pan and add enough water almost to cover the meat. Cover the pan and simmer for about 40 minutes until the meat is tender and the sauce is thick. If the sauce does not thicken sufficiently, remove the lid for the last portion of the cooking time.

5.   Meanwhile, cook the macaroni in boiled salted water until just tender. Drain well and arrange on a warmed serving dish. Top with the lamb stew and serve garnished with parsley.

Serves 4

2 Lamb Steak Parcels

Ingredients

4 large lamb steaks
45 ml/3 tbsp olive oil
Juice of 1 lemon
4 cloves garlic, sliced
15 ml/1 tbsp chopped fresh parsley
Salt and freshly ground black pepper
4 slices hard cheese

Method

1. Arrange the lamb steaks in a large bowl. Mix together the oil, lemon juice, garlic and parsley and season with salt and pepper. Pour over the lamb, cover and leave to marinate for at least 3 hours, turning occasionally.

2. Arrange each lamb steak in a piece of kitchen foil and top with a slice of cheese. Spoon the marinade over the top and seal the foil into parcels. Arrange in a baking dish and bake in a preheated oven at 190°C/375°F/gas mark 5 for about 1 hour until the meat is cooked. Serve with a green salad and potatoes.

Serves 4

3 Lamb Chops with Tomato

Ingredients

4 large lamb chops
3 cloves garlic, chopped
15 ml/1 tbsp chopped fresh rosemary
Salt and freshly ground black pepper
400 g/14 oz canned tomatoes, drained and chopped
150 ml/¹/₄ pt/ ²/₃ cup olive oil

Method

1. Arrange the chops in a single layer in a baking dish. Sprinkle with garlic and rosemary and season with salt and pepper. Pour over the tomatoes and drizzle the olive oil over the top.

2. Bake, uncovered, in a preheated oven at 180°C/350°F/gas mark 4 for about 45 minutes until the chops are tender.

   Serves 4

4 Lamb Kebabs

Ingredients

1.25 kg/3 lb boned leg of lamb, cut into cubes
120 ml/4 fl oz/¹/₂ cup olive oil
Juice of 2 lemons
3 cloves garlic, crushed
10 ml/2 tsp oregano
Salt and freshly ground black pepper
2 onions, cut into wedges
1 red pepper, cut into wedges
1 green pepper, cut into wedges

Method

1. Place the meat in a bowl. Mix together the oil, lemon juice, garlic and oregano and season with salt and pepper. Pour over the meat and stir well. Cover and leave to marinate in the refrigerator overnight.

2. Drain the meat and thread it on to skewers alternately with pieces of onions and pepper. Grill under a preheated grill for about 20 minutes, turning and basting frequently with the marinade.

Serves 4

5 Beef Triangles

Ingredients

225 g/8 oz/1 cup butter or margarine
225 g/8 oz minced beef or veal
1 onion, chopped
100 g/4 oz feta cheese, crumbled
2 eggs, lightly beaten
120 ml/4 fl oz/1/2 cup double cream
Salt and freshly ground black pepper
1 packet filo pastry
1 egg yolk, beaten
50 g/2 oz/1/4 cup sesame seeds

Method

1. Heat 45 ml/3 tbsp of butter or margarine, add the meat and onion and fry for a few minutes until lightly browned. Remove from the heat and leave to cool.

2. Stir in the cheese, eggs and cream and season with salt and pepper.

3. Melt the remaining butter or margarine. Cut the filo pastry into 7.5 cm/3 in strips and brush with butter. Place 1 strip on top of another. Spoon a little of the filling on to the end of a strip and fold over the end of the strip into a triangle. Continue to fold up the strip in a triangle, brush with butter or margarine and place on a greased baking sheet. Continue with the remaining pastry and filling. Brush with egg yolk and sprinkle with sesame seeds.

4. Bake in a preheated oven at 200°C/400°F/gas mark 6 for about 25 minutes until golden brown. Serve hot.

Serves 4

6 Moussaka

Ingredients

450 g/1 lb aubergine, sliced
Salt
250 ml/8 fl oz/1 cup olive oil
2 large onions, chopped
3 cloves garlic, crushed
450 g/1 lb minced beef or lamb
400 g/14 oz canned tomatoes, chopped
45 ml/3 tbsp tomato purée
5 ml/1 tsp ground cinnamon
Salt and freshly ground black pepper
30 ml/2 tbsp butter or margarine
30 ml/2 tbsp plain flour
300 ml/1/2 pt/1 1/4 cups milk
2 eggs, beaten
50 g/2 oz/1/2 cup Parmesan cheese, grated

Method

1. Place the aubergine in a colander and sprinkle generously with salt. Leave for 30 minutes. Rinse in cold water and drain well.

2. Heat half the oil in a frying pan and fry the aubergine slices, a few at a time if necessary, until lightly browned on both sides. Remove from the pan and drain on kitchen paper.

3. Heat the remaining oil and fry the onions and garlic for about 5 minutes until soft. Add the meat and fry until browned. Add the tomatoes, tomato purée and cinnamon and season with salt and pepper. Bring to the boil, cover and simmer gently for about 20 minutes.

4.   Meanwhile, melt the butter or margarine, stir in the flour and cook for 1 minute. Whisk in the milk, bring to the boil, stirring, then simmer for 2 minutes. Remove from the heat, stir in the eggs and Parmesan and season with salt and pepper.

5.   Layer the aubergine, meat sauce and cheese sauce in a shallow baking dish, finishing with a layer of cheese sauce. Bake in a preheated oven at 180°C/350°F/gas mark 4 for about 1 hour until golden brown on top.

Serves 4

7 Cabbage with Mince Stuffing

Ingredients

1 medium cabbage, separated into leaves
Salt
75 ml/5 tbsp olive oil
2 onions, chopped
3 cloves garlic, crushed
225 g/8 oz minced beef
225 g/8 oz minced pork
400 g/14 oz canned tomatoes, chopped
30 ml/2 tbsp chopped fresh parsley
2 eggs, beaten
50 g/2 oz/½ cup Parmesan cheese, grated
Freshly ground black pepper

For the sauce:
60 ml/4 tbsp olive oil
2 onions, sliced
2 cloves garlic, crushed
400 g/14 oz canned tomatoes, chopped
45 ml/3 tbsp tomato purée

Method

1. Blanch the cabbage in boiling salted water for 2 minutes.

2. Heat the oil and fry the onions and garlic for about 4 minutes until just soft. Add the minced meats and stir until well browned. Add the tomatoes and simmer for 20 minutes. Remove from the heat and leave to cool. Stir in the parsley, eggs and cheese and season with salt and pepper.

3. Use the mixture to stuff the cabbage leaves, roll them up tightly and arrange in an ovenproof dish.

4. To make the sauce, heat the oil and fry the onions and garlic for about 5 minutes until soft. Add the tomatoes and tomato purée and season with salt and pepper. Bring to the boil and simmer for about 10 minutes until the sauce thickens, adding a little water if necessary. Pour over the cabbage leaves, cover and bake in a preheated oven at 180°C/350°F/gas mark 4 for about 1 hour.

Serves 4

8 Greek Meatballs

Ingredients

2 slices bread, crusts removed
1 onion, finely chopped
450 g/1 lb minced beef
60 ml/4 tbsp olive oil
2 eggs
45 ml/3 tbsp chopped fresh parsley
15 ml/1 tbsp wine vinegar
5 ml/1 tsp dried oregano
Salt and freshly ground black pepper
50 g/2 oz/½ cup plain flour
Oil for deep-frying

Method

1. Soak the bread in water for about 10 minutes. Drain and squeeze out the excess moisture.

2. Mix together the bread, onion, beef, oil, eggs, parsley, wine vinegar and oregano to make a fairly soft mixture. If it is too stiff, add a little water. Season with salt and pepper. Cover and chill for 2 hours.

3. Roll the mixture into small balls between your hands. Roll in the flour.

4. Heat the oil and fry the meatballs until brown and crisp. Serve at once.

Serves 4

9 Garlic and Beef Sausages

Ingredients

450 g/1 lb minced beef
2 onions, chopped
2 cloves garlic, crushed
60 ml/4 tbsp dried breadcrumbs
15 ml/1 tbsp wine vinegar
60 ml/4 tbsp water
60 ml/4 tbsp olive oil
5 ml/1 tsp dried oregano
Salt and freshly ground black pepper

Method

1. Mix together all the ingredients well and season with salt and pepper. Cover and chill for 3 hours.

2. Roll the mixture into small sausage shapes, brush with a little more oil and grill under a preheated grill for about 15 minutes, turning occasionally, until browned on all sides. Serve with Tzatziki (page 27) or Red Pepper Sauce (page 152).

Serves 4

10 | Meat Loaf in Tomato Sauce

Ingredients

250 ml/8 fl oz/1 cup olive oil
1 onion, chopped
3 cloves garlic, crushed
1 kg/2 lb minced beef
50 g/2 oz/1/2 cup breadcrumbs
15 ml/1 tbsp chopped fresh parsley
15 ml/1 tbsp chopped fresh mint
15 ml/1 tbsp Worcestershire sauce
Salt and freshly ground black pepper
2 eggs, beaten
4 slices Cheddar cheese
Tomato Sauce (page 151)

Method

1. Heat 15 ml/1 tbsp of oil and fry the onion and garlic for about 4 minutes until just soft. Stir in the meat and cook until browned. Remove from the heat and leave to cool a little.

2. Stir in the breadcrumbs, parsley, mint and Worcestershire sauce and season generously with salt and pepper. Bind together with the eggs.

3. Press half the mixture into a greased loaf tin then lay the cheese slices on top. Press in the remaining mixture, making sure the cheese in enclosed in the meat. Pour over the remaining oil.

4. Bake in a preheated oven at 200°C/400°F/gas mark 6 for about 30 minutes until cooked through and brown on top. Serve with tomato sauce.

Serves 4

11 Pork in Red Wine

Ingredients

1.5 kg/3 1/4 lb lean pork, cubed
Salt and freshly ground black pepper
300 ml/ 1/2 pt/1 1/4 cups dry red wine
30 ml/2 tbsp olive oil
5 ml/1 tsp coriander seeds, crushed

Method

1. Place the pork in a deep bowl and sprinkle generously with salt and pepper. Pour over the wine, stir, cover and leave to marinate in a cool place at least overnight.

2. Drain the pork and pat it dry. Heat the oil in a heavy-based saucepan and fry the pork with the coriander until browned on all sides.

3. Add the marinade, cover tightly and simmer gently for about 30 minutes until the meat is tender, stirring and adding a little extra water or wine during cooking if necessary. Serve with boiled potatoes.

Serves 4

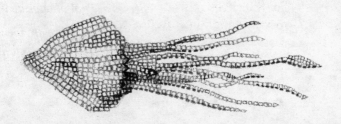

Cheese and Egg Dishes

*Greek cheese and filo pastry pies
are internationally famous.
Although authentic Greek
cheeses are not always available
in Britain, there are plenty of
good substitutes.*

1 Layered Cheese Pie

Ingredients

30 ml/2 tbsp butter or margarine
30 ml/2 tbsp plain flour
300 ml/½ pt/1 ¼ cups milk
2 eggs, beaten
225 g/8 oz/1 cup feta cheese
225 g/8 oz/1 cup cottage cheese
50 g/2 oz/½ cup Parmesan cheese, grated
Salt and freshly ground black pepper
45 ml/3 tbsp olive oil
15 sheets filo pastry
15 ml/1 tbsp sesame seeds

Method

1. Melt the butter or margarine, stir in the flour and cook for 1 minute. Whisk in the milk and simmer until the sauce is thick. Remove from the heat and beat in the eggs a little at a time. Stir in the cheeses and season with salt and pepper.

2. Brush 5 sheets of filo pastry with olive oil and arrange in the base of a greased pie dish. Spoon in one-third of the cheese mixture, top with 5 sheets of oiled filo, the remaining cheese mixture then the remaining oiled pastry. Seal the edges, score the top and sprinkle with a little water and sesame seeds.

3. Bake in a preheated oven at 190°C/375°F/gas mark 5 for about 30 minutes until golden brown.

Serves 4

2 Cheese Puff Turnovers

Ingredients

225 g/8 oz/1 cup feta cheese, crumbled
350 g/12 oz/1 1/2 cups cottage cheese
25 g/1 oz/1/4 cup Parmesan cheese, grated
2 eggs, beaten
5 ml/1 tsp oregano
Salt and freshly ground black pepper
225 g/8 oz puff pastry
15 ml/1 tbsp milk
15 ml/1 tbsp sesame seeds

Method

1. Mix together the cheeses, eggs and oregano and season with salt and pepper.

2. Roll out the pastry and cut into 15 cm/6 in circles. Place spoonfuls of the cheese mixture in the centre of each circle, brush the edges with a little water, fold them over and seal them into semi-circles. Brush the tops with milk and sprinkle with sesame seeds. Bake in a preheated oven at 200°C/400°F/ gas mark 6 for about 20 minutes until golden brown.

Serves 4

3   Eggs with Tomatoes

Ingredients

45 ml/3 tbsp butter or margarine
15 ml/1 tbsp olive oil
2 large tomatoes, thickly sliced
4 eggs
8 black olives, stoned
Salt and freshly ground black pepper

Method

1.   Melt the butter or margarine with the oil in a frying pan. Add the tomatoes and fry until beginning to soften.

2.   Break the eggs into the pan between the tomato slices and add the olives. Season with salt and pepper. Fry gently, spooning the butter over the eggs, until the eggs have just set. Season again with pepper and serve with hot toast.

Serves 4

4 Courgette Omelette

Ingredients

5 courgettes, diced
Salt
75 ml/5 tbsp olive oil
1 onion, chopped
2 cloves garlic, crushed
5 eggs, beaten
15 ml/1 tbsp chopped fresh parsley
Salt and freshly ground black pepper

Method

1. Place the courgettes in a colander and sprinkle generously with salt. Leave to stand for 30 minutes. Rinse in cold water and drain well.

2. Heat the oil and fry the courgettes with the onion and garlic until lightly browned on all sides.

3. Beat the eggs with the parsley and season with salt and pepper. Pour over the courgettes and cook until the base sets, lifting up the base of the omelette so that the uncooked egg can run underneath.

4. Place the pan under a preheated grill for a few minutes to brown the top.

Serves 4

Vegetable
Dishes

*A vegetable hot-pot is a
traditionally popular meal in
Greek households, because it is
economical, nutritious and can
be prepared with whichever
vegetables are at their best.
Always made with olive oil to
give them that traditional
Mediterranean flavour, they
feature delicious rich sauces
flavoured with onions and
tomatoes.*

1 Vegetable Casserole

Ingredients

1 aubergine, cut into chunks
4 courgettes, sliced
Salt
250 ml/8 fl oz/1 cup olive oil
225 g/8 oz potatoes, cut into chunks
2 carrots, sliced
1 green pepper, cut into chunks
225 g/8 oz green beans
225 g/8 oz button mushrooms
3 onions, sliced
2 cloves garlic, crushed
400 g/14 oz canned tomatoes, chopped
45 ml/3 tbsp chopped fresh parsley
Freshly ground black pepper
50 g/2 oz/1/2 cup strong hard cheese, grated

Method

1. Place the aubergine and courgettes in 2 colanders and sprinkle generously with salt. Leave to drain for 30 minutes. Rinse in cold water and pat dry.

2. Heat a little oil and fry the potatoes and carrots until lightly browned. Transfer to a casserole dish.

3. Heating a little more oil each time, fry the peppers, beans and mushrooms in the same way and transfer to the casserole dish.

4. Add the remaining oil to the pan and fry the onions and garlic for about 5 minutes until soft but not browned. Stir in the tomatoes and cook for a further 10 minutes. Stir in the parsley.

5. Pour the sauce over the vegetables and mix together gently. Cover the casserole and bake in a

preheated oven at 180°C/350°F/gas mark 4 for about 45 minutes.

6. Remove the lid and sprinkle with the cheese. Bake for a further 15 minutes until the vegetables are all tender and the sauce is thick. Season well with salt and pepper.

Serves 4

DOLMADES

2 Aubergines with Onions

Ingredients

4 aubergines
Salt
250 ml/8 fl oz/1 cup olive oil
4 onions, sliced
4 cloves garlic
100 g/14 oz canned tomatoes, drained and sieved
45 ml/3 tbsp chopped fresh parsley
Freshly ground black pepper

Method

1. Peel strips of skin lengthways from the aubergines so that they look striped. Cut a slit lengthways down the centre of each one. Sprinkle generously with salt and leave in a colander to drain for 30 minutes. Rinse and pat dry with kitchen paper.

2. Heat half the oil and fry the aubergines for about 5 minutes until golden brown. Transfer to a shallow ovenproof dish.

3. Heat a little more oil and fry the onions and garlic for about 5 minutes until soft. Add the tomatoes and parsley and season with salt and pepper. Bring to the boil and simmer for about 15 minutes.

4. Spoon the tomato mixture into the centre of the aubergines and pour the remaining sauce over the top. Sprinkle with any remaining oil and season well with salt and pepper. Cover and bake in a

preheated oven at 180°C/350°F/gas mark 4 for about 1 hour until tender, adding a little water during cooking if the vegetables begin to dry out.

Serves 4

3 Stuffed Aubergines

Ingredients

2 large aubergines
Salt
120 ml/4 fl oz/½ cup olive oil
2 onions, chopped
2 cloves garlic, chopped
225 g/8 oz minced beef
400 g/14 oz canned tomatoes, chopped
15 ml/1 tbsp chopped fresh parsley
5 ml/1 tsp oregano
Freshly ground black pepper
1 quantity White Sauce (page 147)
1 egg, beaten
50 g/2 oz/½ cup strong cheese, grated
50 g/2 oz/¼ cup butter or margarine, melted

Method

1. Halve the aubergines and scoop out a little of the centre flesh. Sprinkle generously with salt and leave for 30 minutes. Rinse in cold water and drain.

2. Heat the oil and fry the onions and garlic for about 5 minutes until soft. Add the meat and fry until browned. Add the tomatoes, parsley and oregano and season with salt and pepper.

3. Spoon the meat mixture into the aubergine shells and arrange in a single layer in a baking dish.

4. Beat the egg into the white sauce and pour over the aubergines. Sprinkle with cheese and drizzle the melted butter over the top. Bake in a preheated oven at 180°C/350°F/gas mark 4 for about 45 minutes.

5.   Courgettes can be stuffed and cooked in the same way.

Serves 4

4 | Aubergine Fritters

Ingredients

350 g/12 oz/3 cups plain flour
Salt and freshly ground black pepper
2 eggs, separated
175 ml/6 fl oz/ ³/4 cup water
2 aubergines, sliced
Olive oil for frying

Method

1. Season the flour with salt and pepper. Mix in the egg yolks and water, cover and leave to chill for 1 hour.

2. Arrange the aubergines in a colander, sprinkle generously with salt and leave to drain for 30 minutes. Rinse in cold water and pat dry on kitchen paper.

3. Beat the egg whites until stiff then fold them into the batter.

4. Heat the oil. Dip the aubergine slices in the batter until well coated and fry in the hot oil until golden brown on both sides. Drain on kitchen paper before serving with Garlic and Potato Sauce (page 149).

Serves 4

5 Broad Beans with Onions

Ingredients

1 kg/2 lb broad beans
120 ml/4 fl oz/ 1/2 cup olive oil
3 spring onions, chopped
5 ml/1 tsp sugar
Salt and freshly ground black pepper
15 ml/1 tbsp chopped fresh dill
1 lemon, cut into wedges
30 ml/2 tbsp Greek yoghurt

Method

1. Shell the beans and rinse in cold water.

2. Heat the oil in a large saucepan and fry the onions for about 4 minutes until soft.

3. Add the beans and sugar and season with salt and pepper. Pour over enough hot water to cover the beans, bring to the boil, cover and simmer for about 20 minutes, stirring occasionally, until the liquid has thickened.

4. Transfer to a warmed serving dish, sprinkle with dill, place the lemon wedges round the edge of the dish and garnish with the yoghurt.

Serves 4

6 Buttered Carrots

Ingredients

450 g/1 lb carrots, cubed
Salt
75 g/3 oz/ ^{1}/$_3$ cup butter or margarine
15 ml/1 tbsp lemon juice
Freshly ground black pepper

Method

1. Cook the carrots in boiling salted water for about 10 minutes until just tender.

2. Drain well, return to the hot saucepan and toss over a gentle heat until dry.

3. Add the butter or margarine and toss together carefully until the carrots are coated in the melted butter.

4. Add the lemon juice and season well with salt and pepper.

Serves 4

7 | Courgettes with Garlic and Cheese

Ingredients

12 small courgettes
12 cloves garlic, crushed
250 ml/8 fl oz/1 cup olive oil
45 ml/3 tbsp chopped fresh parsley
5 ml/1 tsp paprika
Salt and freshly ground black pepper
100 g/4 oz feta cheese, cubed

Method

1. Cut the courgettes in half lengthways and scoop out the seeds. Arrange, cut sides up, in a shallow ovenproof dish.

2. Mix together the garlic, oil, parsley and paprika and season with salt and pepper. Spoon the mixture into the courgette shells then spoon any remaining dressing over the top.

3. Arrange the feta cheese in the courgette shells and season again with salt and pepper. Cover with foil and bake in a preheated oven at 180°C/350°F/gas mark 4 for about 1¼ hours until tender. Serve hot or cold.

Serves 4

8 Garlic Mushrooms

Ingredients

450 g/1 lb mushrooms, sliced
450 g/1 lb tomatoes, skinned and chopped
6 cloves garlic, crushed
150 ml/¼ pt/⅔ cup olive oil
15 ml/1 tbsp chopped fresh parsley
5 ml/1 tsp dried oregano
5 ml/1 tsp lemon juice
Salt and freshly ground black pepper

Method

1. Mix together the mushrooms, tomatoes and garlic and arrange in an ovenproof dish.

2. Mix the oil, parsley, oregano and lemon juice and season with salt and pepper. Pour over the vegetables and toss lightly. Season again with salt and pepper.

3. Cover and bake in a preheated oven at 180°C/350°F/gas mark 4 for about 45 minutes until the mushrooms are soft and most of the liquid has been absorbed.

Serves 4

9 | Deep-Fried Mushrooms

Ingredients

450 g/1 lb button mushrooms
50 g/2 oz/¹/₂ cup plain flour
5ml/1tsp cayenne pepper
Salt and freshly ground black pepper
Olive oil for deep-frying
1 lemon, cut into wedges

Method

1. Trim the mushrooms if necessary. Season the flour generously with cayenne pepper, salt and pepper and place it in a plastic bag. Add the mushrooms and shake until well coated. Transfer to a sieve and shake off any excess flour.

2. Heat the oil and deep-fry the mushrooms for a few minutes until golden and crispy. Garnish with lemon and serve at once.

Serves 4

10 | Okra with Tomatoes

Ingredients

450 g/1 lb okra
Salt
15 ml/1 tbsp white wine vinegar
150 ml/¹/₄ pt/ ²/₃ cup olive oil
1 onion, finely chopped
1 clove garlic, crushed
400 g/14 oz canned tomatoes, drained and sieved
45 ml/3 tbsp chopped fresh parsley
A few lemon slices
A pinch of sugar
2 tomatoes, sliced
Freshly ground black pepper

Method

1. Place the okra in a saucepan, sprinkle with salt and leave to stand for 30 minutes. Rinse and drain the okra thoroughly and toss with the wine vinegar.

2. Heat the oil and fry the onion and garlic for about 5 minutes until soft but not browned. Add the okra, tomatoes, parsley, lemon slices and sugar, bring to the boil and simmer for 10 minutes.

3. Arrange the tomato slices on top and season with salt and pepper, partially cover and simmer gently for about 10 minutes until tender, shaking the pan occasionally.

Serves 4

11 Peas with Tomatoes

Ingredients

120 ml/4 fl oz/ 1/2 cup olive oil
3 spring onions, chopped
1 kg/2 lb peas, shelled
400 g/14 oz canned tomatoes, drained and chopped
30 ml/2 tbsp chopped fresh dill
Salt and freshly ground black pepper

Method

1. Heat the oil in a large saucepan and fry the onions for about 4 minutes until soft.

2. Stir in the peas until well covered with oil and fry until lightly coloured.

3. Add the tomatoes and dill and season with salt and pepper. Just cover the peas with hot water, bring to the boil and simmer for about 20 minutes until the water has evaporated and the peas are tender.

Serves 4

12 Spinach Pie

Ingredients

675 g/1 1/2 lb spinach
Salt
120 ml/4 fl oz/ 1/2 cup olive oil
2 spring onions, chopped
1 onion, chopped
3 sprigs of dill or mint, finely chopped
3 sprigs of parsley, finely chopped
Freshly ground black pepper
100 g/4 oz feta cheese, crumbled
2 eggs, beaten
8 sheets filo pastry
100 g/4 oz butter, melted

Method

1. Shred the spinach into a saucepan and add just a very little water. Cover and heat until wilted then cool.

2. Heat the oil and fry the spring onions and onions for about 5 minutes until soft. Add the dill and parsley and season with salt and pepper. Cover and simmer for about 10 minutes. Remove from the heat and leave to cool.

3. Stir in the cheese, eggs and spinach.

4. Brush the filo pastry sheets with melted butter and arrange half of them in the base of a greased pie dish. Spoon in the spinach mixture and top with the remaining pastry. Seal the edges and brush with melted butter. Score a pattern through the top sheet of pastry.

5. Bake in a preheated oven at 180°C/350°F/gas mark 4 for about 35 minutes until crisp and golden brown. Serve hot or cold.

Serves 4

13 Fried Potato Cakes

Ingredients

900 g/2 lb potatoes
1 onion, finely chopped
2 eggs, beaten
75 g/3 oz/ ¾ cup strong cheese, grated
15 ml/1 tbsp chopped fresh parsley
Salt and freshly ground black pepper
50 g/2 oz/ ½ cup plain flour
60 ml/4 tbsp olive oil

Method

1. Cook the potatoes in boiling salted water until tender. Drain, peel and mash or purée.

2. Mix the mashed potatoes with the onion, eggs, cheese and parsley and season well with salt and pepper. Mix the ingredients thoroughly and shape into small balls or patties. Chill for 2 hours.

3. Coat the potato cakes in flour. Heat the oil and fry the cakes for about 5 minutes each side until crispy and golden brown. Serve with grilled meats.

Serves 4

14 | Crispy-Fried Potatoes

Ingredients

450 g/1 lb potatoes
Olive oil for deep-frying
Salt
50 g/2 oz/¹/2 cup strong cheese, grated

Method

1. Slice the potatoes very thinly, rinse well under running water, drain and pat dry.

2. Heat the oil and deep-fry the potatoes a few at a time until crisp and golden. Arrange on a warmed serving plate and keep them warm while you fry the remainder.

3. Season generously with salt and sprinkle with cheese before serving.

Serves 4

Pulses and Rice

General Notes

Pulses are popular in Greece, both as a base for main meals, as vegetable dishes or in conjunction with many varieties of fresh vegetables.

They are not difficult to prepare, although they do require a little forethought as the dried pulses which are available in Britain need soaking overnight in cold water before cooking. In many cases the pulses are then boiled for about 1 hour to tenderise them before completing the cooking with the other ingredients in the recipe.

Remember that red kidney beans must be boiled vigorously for 15 minutes during the cooking process to destroy the toxins they contain.

If you do not have time to presoak and cook pulses, take advantage of the many canned varieties which are now available. Simply drain and rinse them and add them to the dish towards the end of cooking time.

Many varieties of rice are popular in Greece but for most rice dishes, Greeks would use a medium-grain rice rather than the long-grain types which are more popular in Britain. Look for a rice marked medium-grain, arborio, Italian or risotto for these dishes.

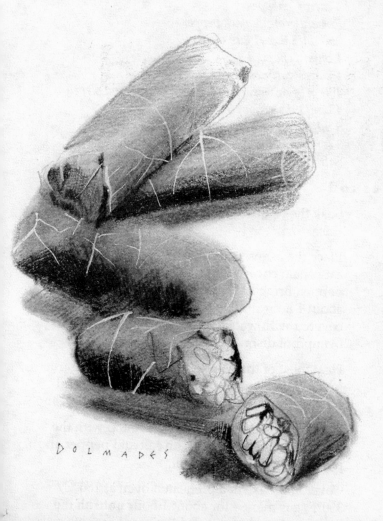

DOLMADES

Baked Butter Beans

Ingredients

350 g/12 oz dried butter beans
2 sticks celery, chopped
1 carrot, chopped
Freshly ground black pepper
250 ml/8 fl oz/1 cup olive oil
1 onion, chopped
4 cloves garlic, crushed
400 g/14 oz canned tomatoes, drained and sieved
45 ml/3 tbsp chopped fresh parsley
5 ml/1 tsp dried oregano
3 tomatoes, sliced
Salt

Method

1. Soak the beans overnight in cold water. Drain and rinse.

2. Place the beans, celery and carrot in a large saucepan, cover with cold water and season with pepper. Bring to the boil, cover and simmer for about 1 hour until tender, keeping the beans covered with water. Drain and transfer to an ovenproof dish.

3. Heat most of the oil and fry the onion and garlic for 5 minutes until soft. Add the tomatoes and bring to a simmer. Stir in the parsley and oregano.

4. Pour the sauce over the beans and top with the sliced tomatoes. Season with salt and pepper and pour over the remaining oil.

5. Cover and bake in a preheated oven at 180°C/350°F/gas mark 4 for about 1 hour until all the liquid has evaporated and the beans are soft.

Check the dish occasionally and add a little hot water if the liquid dries out before the beans are soft.

Serves 4

2 Stuffed Cabbage Rolls

Ingredients

1 small cabbage
Salt
250 ml/8 fl oz/1 cup olive oil
1 large onion, chopped
200 g/7 oz canned tomatoes, drained and sieved
45 ml/3 tbsp chopped fresh parsley
2.5 ml/1/2 tsp paprika
15 ml/1 tbsp lemon juice
Freshly ground black pepper
225 g/8 oz/1 cup medium-grain rice

Method

1. Cut the cabbage around the core then cook it in boiling salted water for about 10 minutes. Drain well then remove the cabbage leaves.

2. Heat the oil and fry the onion for about 5 minutes until soft. Stir in the tomatoes, parsley, paprika and lemon juice and season with salt and pepper. Bring to the boil then simmer for 15 minutes.

3. Stir in the rice then strain the sauce, reserving the juice.

4. Place spoonfuls of the stuffing mixture on each cabbage leaf, fold over the edges then roll them up, enclosing the filling. Arrange the leaves, seams downwards, in a shallow ovenproof dish. Pour over the reserved sauce and season again with salt and pepper.

5. Cover tightly and bake in a preheated oven at 180°C/350°F/gas mark 4 for about 1 hour until the

rice is tender and the liquid has been absorbed, adding a little hot water during cooking if necessary.

Serves 4

3 Chick Peas with Aubergine

Ingredients

450 g/1 lb dried chick peas
5 ml/1 tsp bicarbonate of soda
1 onion, chopped
250 ml/8 fl oz/1 cup olive oil
A pinch of cayenne pepper
Salt and freshly ground black pepper
2 aubergines, sliced

Method

1. Soak the chick peas overnight in cold water with the bicarbonate of soda. Drain and rub off the skins.

2. Place the chick peas in a saucepan and almost cover with cold water. Add the onion, 60 ml/4 tbsp of oil and season with cayenne pepper, salt and pepper. Bring to the boil, skim, cover and simmer for about 1 hour until tender and thick.

3. Meanwhile, place the aubergines in a colander, sprinkle generously with salt and leave to drain for 30 minutes. Rinse the aubergines and pat dry on kitchen paper.

4. Heat the remaining oil and fry the aubergines until crispy and golden brown. Drain well on kitchen paper.

5. Arrange the aubergines on top of the chick peas, remove the lid and continue to simmer for a further 10 minutes.

Serves 4

4 Stuffed Peppers

Ingredients

4 large peppers
250 ml/8 fl oz/1 cup olive oil
2 potatoes, cut into chunks
1 onion, chopped
1 clove garlic, crushed
200 g/7 oz canned tomatoes, drained and sieved
30 ml/2 tbsp tomato purée
Salt and freshly ground black pepper
225 g/8 oz/1 cup medium-grain rice
15 ml/1 tbsp chopped fresh mint
15 ml/1 tbsp chopped fresh parsley

Method

1. Slice off and reserve the pepper tops and scoop out the seeds and pith. Stand the peppers upright in an ovenproof dish.

2. Heat a little oil and fry the potatoes until golden brown. Arrange around the peppers.

3. Heat a little more oil in the pan and fry the onion and garlic for about 5 minutes until soft. Stir in the tomatoes and tomato purée and season with salt and pepper. Bring to the boil and simmer for 15 minutes.

4. Stir in the rice, mint and parsley and spoon the mixture into the peppers. Replace the tops. Cover tightly and bake in a preheated oven at 180°C/350°F/gas mark 4 for about 1¹/₂ hours until the peppers are tender and the rice is cooked, adding a little boiling water while baking, if necessary.

Serves 4

Salads and Salad Dressings

General Notes

Every Greek meal is accompanied by a salad to complement the main course, whether it is a salad of lightly cooked fresh vegetables, a marinated salad or a raw salad of tomatoes and salad leaves. The ingredients are always fresh and perfect and prepared carefully to maximise their flavour and nutritional value. Tossing them together gently at the last minute with a simple dressing of olive oil and wine vinegar maintains their flavour and crispness. A little salt and pepper and perhaps a touch of fresh herbs such as parsley, mint, basil, rosemary or thyme complete the picture.

You can use any kind of salad ingredients you like and be creative with all the new types of lettuce now available in the supermarkets to give a contrast of crisp and softer leaves, mild tasting and more piquant varieties. Onions, tomatoes, olives and beans are very popular in Greek salads, but don't forget cabbage, quickly blanched cauliflower, spinach, peppers, cucumber and mushrooms.

1 Mixed Greek Salad

Ingredients

1 cucumber, sliced
1 onion, sliced
2 tomatoes, cut into wedges
100 g/4 oz feta cheese, cubed
1 hard-boiled egg, cut into wedges
8 black olives, stoned
250 ml/8 fl oz/1 cup Oil and Vinegar Dressing (page 130)
Salt and freshly ground black pepper

Method

1. Mix together the cucumber, onion, tomatoes and cheese. Arrange the egg and olives on top.

2. Just before serving, spoon the dressing over the salad and toss gently. Season with salt and pepper.

Serves 4

2 Carrot Salad

Ingredients

5 carrots, grated
15 ml/1 tbsp grated onion
5 ml/1 tsp capers
3 radishes, sliced
250 ml/8 fl oz/1 cup Oil and Lemon Dressing (page
131)

Method

1. Mix together the carrots, onion, capers and radishes.

2. Just before serving, spoon the dressing over the salad and toss gently. Season with salt and pepper.

Serves 4

3 Chick Pea Salad

Ingredients

350 g/12 oz/2 cups dried chick peas
5 ml/1 tsp bicarbonate of soda
2 onions, chopped
45 ml/3 tbsp chopped fresh parsley
90 ml/6 tbsp olive oil
60 ml/4 tbsp wine vinegar
Salt and freshly ground black pepper

Method

1. Soak the chick peas overnight in cold water with the bicarbonate of soda. Drain and rinse well.

2. Place the chick peas in a saucepan, cover with fresh water, bring to the boil, cover the pan and simmer for about 1 hour until tender. Top up with cold water during cooking if necessary to keep the peas covered.

3. Drain the peas, turn into a salad bowl and leave to cool.

4. Mix together the remaining ingredients and pour over the chick peas. Toss well and chill before serving.

Serves 4

4 Courgette Salad

Ingredients

6 small courgettes
Salt
1 sprig mint
300 ml/ 1/2 pt/1 1/4 cups mayonnaise
Freshly ground black pepper

Method

1. Trim the courgettes and cut into julienne strips. Bring a saucepan of salted water to the boil with the mint. Toss in the courgette strips and blanch for about 2 minutes. Drain and rinse in cold water.

2. Arrange the courgettes in a salad bowl and mix with the mayonnaise. Season with salt and pepper and chill before serving.

Serves 4

5 Cucumber and Tomato Salad

Ingredients

1 cucumber, sliced
3 tomatoes, cut into wedges
1 green pepper, chopped
45 ml/3 tbsp chopped fresh parsley
1 clove garlic, crushed
250 ml/8 fl oz/1 cup Oil and Vinegar Dressing (page 130)
Salt and freshly ground black pepper

Method

1. Mix together the cucumber, tomatoes, pepper and parsley.

2. Mix the garlic into the dressing.

3. Just before serving, spoon the dressing over the salad and toss gently. Season with salt and pepper.

Serves 4

6 Mushrooms in Ouzo

Ingredients

225 g/8 oz mushrooms, sliced
8 black olives, stoned
60 ml/4 tbsp olive oil
30 ml/2 tbsp ouzo
45 ml/3 tbsp chopped fresh parsley
1 clove garlic, crushed
Juice of 1/2 lemon
5 ml/1 tsp oregano
2.5 ml/1/2 tsp chopped red chilli pepper
Salt and freshly ground black pepper

Method

1. Mix together the mushrooms and olives.

2. Mix together the remaining ingredients and season with salt and pepper. Pour over the mushrooms and mix together gently.

3. Cover and chill before serving.

Serves 4

7 Potato Salad

Ingredients

450 g/1 lb potatoes
Salt
1 carrot, sliced
1 onion, sliced
4 spring onions, chopped
45 ml/3 tbsp chopped fresh mint
75 ml/5 tbsp olive oil
60 ml/4 tbsp white wine vinegar
2.5 ml/1/2 tsp mild mustard
Freshly ground black pepper

Method

1. Cook the potatoes in boiling salted water until tender. Drain and rinse under cold water. Peel and cut into cubes. Blanch the carrot in boiling salted water for a few minutes. Drain well.

2. Mix the potatoes, carrots, onion and spring onions.

3. Mix together the mint, olive oil, wine vinegar and mustard and season with salt and pepper. Spoon the dressing over the salad, toss gently and chill for 1 hour.

4. Toss again and season with salt and pepper before serving.

Serves 4

8 Prawn and Olive Salad

Ingredients

450 g/1 lb cooked peeled prawns
8 black olives, stoned
75 ml/5 tbsp olive oil
Juice of 1 large lemon
45 ml/3 tbsp chopped fresh parsley
Salt and freshly ground black pepper

Method

1. Mix together the prawns and olives.

2. Thoroughly mix the olive oil, lemon juice and parsley and season with salt and pepper.

3. Toss the salad in the dressing, cover and chill well before serving.

Serves 4

9 Rice Salad

Ingredients

450 g/1 lb cooked rice
2 gherkins, chopped
100 g/4 oz salami, chopped
1 onion, chopped
1/2 red pepper, chopped
1 carrot, grated
100 g/4 oz canned sweetcorn, drained
100 g/4 oz cooked peas
6 olives, stoned and chopped
30 ml/2 tbsp chopped fresh parsley
75 ml/5 tbsp olive oil
Juice of 1 lemon
15 ml/1 tbsp white wine vinegar
Salt and freshly ground black pepper

Method

1. Mix together the rice, gherkins, salami, onion, pepper, carrot, sweetcorn, peas and olives.

2. Thoroughly mix the parsley, olive oil, lemon juice and wine vinegar and season with salt and pepper.

3. Mix the dressing thoroughly into the rice then press the mixture into a ring tin. Chill thoroughly.

4. Turn out on to a serving plate and serve with cold meats

Serves 4-6

10 | Tomato and Onion Salad

Ingredients

4 tomatoes, cut into wedges
1 large onion, sliced
15 ml/1 tbsp chopped fresh oregano
250 ml/8 fl oz/1 cup Oil and Vinegar Dressing (page 130)
Salt and freshly ground black pepper

Method

1. Mix together the tomatoes, onions and oregano.

2. Just before serving, spoon the dressing over the salad and toss gently. Season with salt and pepper.

Serves 4

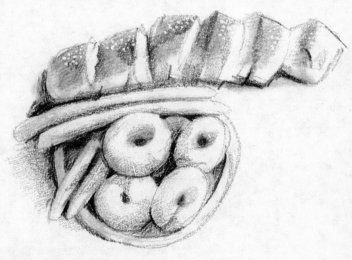

Oil and Vinegar Dressing

Ingredients

> 150 ml/ ¼ pt/ ⅔ cup olive oil
> 75 ml/5 tbsp white wine vinegar
> 5 ml/1 tsp mild mustard
> 2.5 ml/ ½ tsp dried oregano
> Salt and freshly ground black pepper

Method

1. Place all the ingredients into a screw-top jar and shake until well blended, seasoning to taste with salt and pepper.

   Makes 250 ml/8 fl oz/1 cup

12 Oil and Lemon Dressing

Ingredients

150 ml/¼ pt/¾ cup olive oil
75 ml/5 tbsp lemon juice
5 ml/1 tsp oregano
5 ml/1 tsp chopped fresh parsley
Salt and freshly ground black pepper

Method

1. Place all the ingredients into a screw-top jar and shake until well blended, seasoning to taste with salt and pepper.

Makes 250 ml/8 fl oz/1 cup

Desserts
and Cakes

*Fruit is the most popular dessert
in Greece and there is not a broad
culinary tradition of serving
elaborate desserts. To serve your
fruits in Greek style, they should
be peeled, sliced and arranged
attractively on a serving plate
sprinkled with a little sugar or
cinnamon. Guests help
themselves using little forks or
cocktail sticks.*

1 Baklava

Ingredients

200 g/7 oz/1 ³/₄ cups almonds, finely chopped
300 g/10 oz/2 ¹/₂ cups walnuts, finely chopped
100 g/4 oz/ ¹/₂ cup caster sugar
10 ml/2 tsp ground cinnamon
A pinch of ground cloves
200 g/7 oz/ ³/₄ cup butter or margarine, melted
30 sheets filo pastry

For the syrup:
750 g/1 ¹/₂ lb/3 cups caster sugar
600 ml/1 pt/2 ¹/₂ cups water
2 cinnamon sticks
150 g/5 oz/ ¹/₂ cup honey
45 ml/3 tbsp lemon juice
5 cloves
A strip of lemon rind

Method

1. Mix together the nuts, sugar, cinnamon and cloves.

2. Brush a 33 x 23 cm/13 x 9 in baking tin and 10 sheets of filo pastry with butter or margarine. Line the bottom of the dish with the pastry.

3. Spread one-third of the nut mixture evenly on top. Brush 5 more sheets of filo with butter or margarine and arrange them on top. Repeat until you have used all the ingredients.

4. Trim and seal the edges of the pastry, score through the top layers in a diamond pattern and sprinkle with water. Bake in a preheated oven at 180°C/350°F/gas mark 4 for 40 minutes until golden brown.

5.   Meanwhile, mix together all the syrup ingredients over a low heat, stirring until the sugar dissolves. Bring to the boil and boil for 8 minutes. Strain and leave to cool.

6.   Pour the syrup over the hot baklava and leave to stand overnight before serving.

Serves 6-8

2 Honey Puffs

Ingredients

10 ml/2 tsp dried yeast
600 ml/1 pt/2 1/2 cups warm water
5 ml/1 tsp sugar
450 g/1 lb/4 cups plain flour
450 g/1 lb/1 1/2 cups honey
75 ml/5 tbsp water
Oil for deep-frying
Ground cinnamon
Icing sugar

Method

1. Dissolve the yeast in a little warm water with the sugar and leave in a warm place until frothy.

2. Sift the flour into a bowl and add the yeast mixture and remaining warm water. Knead until smooth then continue to knead until elastic. Cover with oiled clingfilm and set aside in a warm place for about 2 hours until doubled in size.

3. Mix together the honey and water and leave over a very gentle heat.

4. Heat the oil and drop in tablespoonfuls of the dough a few at a time. Fry for a few minutes until puffed and golden brown. Dip in the hot honey mixture and arrange on a warmed serving plate. Sprinkle with cinnamon and icing sugar and serve warm.

Serves 4

3 Rum Baba

Ingredients

For the syrup:
225 g/8 oz/1 cup sugar
90 ml/6 tbsp water
90 ml/6 tbsp cup rum
A strip of lemon rind

2 eggs
100 g/4 oz/¹/₂ cup caster sugar
2.5 ml/¹/₂ tsp vanilla essence
100 g/4 oz/1 cup plain flour
5 ml/1 tsp baking powder

Method

1. To make the syrup, boil all the ingredients together for 4 minutes. Leave to cool then strain.

2. Beat the eggs thoroughly then beat in the sugar until light and fluffy. Beat in the vanilla essence, flour and baking powder.

3. Pour into a greased ring cake tin or individual ring moulds and bake in a preheated oven at 180°C/350°F/gas mark 4 for about 35 minutes for a single baba or 20 minutes for individual ones.

4. Pour the syrup over the hot baba and leave to stand for at least 3 hours before serving with whipped cream.

Serves 4

4 Greek Rice Pudding

Ingredients

175 g/6 oz/ ¾ cup short-grain rice
750 ml/1 ¼ pt/3 cups water
750 ml/1 ¼ pt/3 cups milk
100 g/4 oz/ ½ cup caster sugar
5 ml/1 tsp vanilla essence
Ground cinnamon

Method

1. Place the rice, water, milk, sugar and vanilla essence in a saucepan and bring slowly to the boil, stirring until the sugar has dissolved.

2. Simmer over a low heat for about 30 minutes until thick. Sprinkle with cinnamon and serve warm or cold.

Serves 4

5 Pears in Red Wine

Ingredients

4 hard pears, peeled and halved
100 g/4 oz prunes, stoned
250 ml/8 fl oz/1 cup sweet red wine
A strip of lemon rind
1 stick cinnamon

Method

1. Place all the ingredients in a saucepan. Bring to the boil slowly, cover and simmer for about 20 minutes until the pears are tender and the prunes swollen, adding a little more water or wine during cooking if necessary. Remove the cinnamon and lemon rind.

2. Leave to cool then chill and serve with cream or yoghurt.

Serves 4

6 Almond Bicuits

Ingredients

> 100 g/4 oz/1 cup almonds
> 5 ml/1 tsp olive oil
> 225 g/8 oz/1 cup butter or margarine
> 25 g/1 oz/¼ cup icing sugar
> 30 ml/2 tbsp ouzo
> 5 ml/1 tsp vanilla essence
> 1 egg yolk
> 400 g/14 oz/3 ½ cups plain flour
> 5 ml/1 tsp baking powder
> Icing sugar for dusting

Method

1. Mix together the almonds and oil in a heavy-based pan until the almonds are well coated. Heat over a gentle heat, shaking the pan, until the almonds are light golden. Crush the nuts.

2. Melt the butter or margarine and heat gently until the colour begins to darken. Pour into a bowl and leave to cool.

3. Beat the butter or margarine. Add the icing sugar, ouzo and vanilla essence and beat well.

4. Beat in the egg yolk and almonds then gradually work in the flour and baking powder until you have a workable dough; you may not need all the flour.

5. Shape into crescents and place on ungreased baking trays. Bake in a preheated oven at 180°C/350°F/gas mark 4 for about 15 minutes. Leave to cool for a few minutes on the tray.

6. Dust some greaseproof paper generously with icing sugar and place the biscuits on the paper. Dust with icing sugar and leave to cool.

Makes 24

7 Dried Fruit Salad

Ingredients

100 g/4 oz/ ³/4 cup dried apricots
4 prunes, stoned
4 dried peach halves
2 dried figs, halved
50 g/2 oz sultanas
50 g/2 oz almonds
1 stick cinnamon
450 ml/ ³/4 pt/2 cups hot tea
Sugar to taste
150 ml/ ¹/4 pt/ ²/3 cup Greek yoghurt

Method

1. Arrange the dried fruits and nuts in a large bowl, using whatever selection you prefer. Pour over the hot tea and leave to stand overnight.

2. Transfer the fruit to a saucepan and add a little more water, if necessary. Add sugar to taste and bring to the boil slowly, stirring until the sugar dissolves. Simmer gently until the fruit is soft then leave to cool and chill.

3. Serve with a swirl of yoghurt on the top.

Serves 4

8 Greek Cheese Tarts

Ingredients

450 g/1 lb/4 cups plain flour
120 ml/4 fl oz/1/2 cup olive oil
90 ml/6 tbsp water
250 g/9 oz Mascarpone or soft cream cheese
3 eggs, beaten
5 ml/1 tsp vanilla essence
15 ml/1 tbsp butter or margarine
15 ml/1 tbsp semolina
225 g/8 oz/1 cup caster sugar
15 ml/1 tbsp ground cinnamon

Method

1. Sift the flour into a bowl and stir in the olive oil. Add just enough water to make a smooth pastry. Roll out the pastry, cut into squares and use to line greased bun tins.

2. Mix together the cheese, eggs, vanilla essence, butter or margarine, semolina and sugar. Spoon the mixture into the pastry cases and lift the corners to hold in the filling. Sprinkle with cinnamon.

3. Bake the tarts in a preheated oven at 180°C/350°F/ gas mark 4 for about 35 minutes until firm and golden.

Serves 4-6

9 Honey Cakes

Ingredients

225 g/8 oz/1 cup butter, softened
175 g/6 oz/ ³/₄ cup caster sugar
2 egg yolks
Grated rind of 1 orange
450 g/1 lb/4 cups plain flour
10 ml/2 tsp baking powder
75 ml/5 tbsp orange juice
1 egg, beaten

Method

1. Cream the butter and sugar. Mix in the egg yolks and orange rind then the flour, baking powder and orange juice. Add a little milk, if necessary, to make a stiff dough.

2. Roll out the dough into small balls and flatten them on to a greased baking sheet with the back of a fork. Brush with beaten egg.

3. Bake in a preheated oven at 180°C/350°F/gas mark 4 for about 20 minutes until golden.

Serves 4

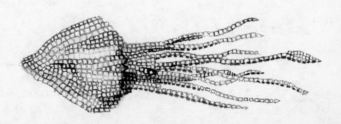

10 Celebration Corn Bread

Ingredients

350 g/12 oz/3 cups polenta
100 g/4 oz/1 cup plain flour
30 ml/2 tbsp baking powder
5 ml/1 tsp salt
120 ml/4 fl oz/1/2 cup olive oil
250 ml/8 fl oz/1 cup orange juice
Grated rind of 2 oranges
75 ml/5 tbsp brandy
175 g/6 oz/1 cup currants
50 g/2 oz/1/4 cup caster sugar
175 ml/6 fl oz/3/4 cup water
45 ml/3 tbsp honey

Method

1. Stir together the polenta, flour, baking powder and salt in a large bowl.

2. Warm the olive oil and mix it into the dry ingredients, using your fingers if necessary.

3. Make a well in the centre and add the orange juice and rind, brandy, currants and sugar. Add just enough water to make a thick batter mixture.

4. Pour the mixture into a greased baking tin and bake in a preheated oven at 180°C/350°F/gas mark 4 for about 40 minutes until golden brown and firm.

5. Leave to cool in the tin for a few minutes then brush with honey.

Serves 4

Sauces

*Many Greek dishes come
complete with their own sauces,
but these traditional sauces can
accompany many main courses
or be used to add piquancy and
Greek style to a simple meat or
fish dish.*

1 White Sauce

Ingredients

30 ml/2 tbsp butter or margarine
30 ml/2 tbsp plain flour
250 ml/8 fl oz/1 cup milk
A pinch of grated nutmeg
Salt and freshly ground black pepper

Method

1. Melt the butter or margarine, add the flour and cook gently for 1 minute without allowing the mixture to brown.

2. Stir in the milk, bring to the boil and simmer for 3 minutes, stirring continuously until the sauce is thick and smooth.

3. Season with nutmeg, salt and pepper.

4. For a thicker sauce, use 45 ml/3 tbsp each of butter or margarine and flour.

5. You can flavour this basic sauce with all kinds of ingredients: chopped hard-boiled eggs, chopped anchovies; tomato ketchup; chopped fresh parsley; chopped capers. You can make an onion sauce by frying chopped onions with the butter before adding the flour.

Serves 4

2 | Egg and Lemon Sauce

This is used as a thickening and flavouring sauce for soups, in which case you can take the stock from the dish you are cooking.

Ingredients

2 eggs, beaten
Juice of 1 large lemon
250 ml/8 fl oz/1 cup chicken or vegetable stock

Method

1. Beat the eggs then add the lemon juice.

2. Warm the stock and stir a little into the egg mixture.

3. Pour the mixture into the soup or stew, stirring continuously, and leave over the lowest heat. Stir until the mixture has thickened.

Serves 4

3 Garlic and Potato Sauce

Ingredients

2 cooked potatoes, mashed
5 cloves garlic, crushed
5 ml/1 tsp salt
30 ml/2 tbsp hot water
120 ml/4 fl oz/1/2 cup olive oil
60 ml/4 tbsp lemon juice

Method

1. Beat together the potatoes, garlic, salt and water.

2. Gradually blend in the oil and lemon juice and beat well. Chill before serving.

Serves 4

Meat Sauce

Serve this sauce with rice or pasta.

Ingredients

45 ml/3 tbsp olive oil
3 onions, finely chopped
2 cloves garlic, crushed
450 g/1 lb minced beef
120 ml/4 fl oz/1/2 cup dry red wine
400 g/14 oz canned tomatoes, chopped
45 ml/3 tbsp tomato purée
1 bay leaf
2.5 ml/1/2 tsp sugar
2.5 ml/1/2 tsp ground cinnamon
A pinch of grated nutmeg
Salt and freshly ground black pepper

Method

1. Heat the oil and fry the onions and garlic gently for about 5 minutes until soft. Add the meat and stir until sealed and browned on all sides. Add the wine and simmer for 2 minutes. Add the tomatoes, tomato purée, bay leaf, sugar, cinnamon and nutmeg and season with salt and pepper. Cover and simmer gently for about 1 hour.

2. You can thin the sauce by adding a little more water, if you wish, or thicken it by simmering without a lid at the end of cooking time.

Serves 4

5 Tomato Sauce

Ingredients

60 ml/4 tbsp olive oil
1 onion, finely chopped
2 cloves garlic, crushed
900 g/2 lb tomatoes, skinned, seeded and chopped
30 ml/2 tbsp tomato purée
15 ml/1 tbsp white wine vinegar
5 ml/1 tsp sugar
15 ml/1 tbsp chopped fresh parsley
Salt and freshly ground black pepper

Method

1. Heat the oil and fry the onion and garlic for about 5 minutes until soft but not browned.

2. Add the tomatoes, tomato purée, wine vinegar and sugar, cover and simmer gently for about 20 minutes until thick.

3. Add the parsley and season with salt and pepper.

4. Serve with meat, vegetables or pasta.

Serves 4

6 | Red Pepper Sauce

Ingredients

> 900 g/2 lb tomatoes, skinned, seeded and chopped
> 120 ml/4 fl oz/1/2 cup olive oil
> 4 cloves garlic, chopped
> 30 ml/2 tbsp chopped fresh parsley
> 450 g/1 lb canned red peppers, drained and chopped
> Cayenne pepper
> Salt and freshly ground black pepper

Method

1. Place the tomatoes, oil, garlic and parsley in a saucepan and bring to the boil. Simmer gently for about 30 minutes, stirring occasionally, until the liquid has evaporated.

2. Add the peppers and season with cayenne pepper, salt and pepper. Continue to simmer, stirring occasionally, until the sauce is thick and pulpy. Remove from the heat and leave to cool.

3. Store the sauce in a screw-top jar in the refrigerator.

Serves 4

7 Spiced Mayonnaise

Ingredients

> 250 ml/8 fl oz/1 cup mayonnaise
> 5 ml/1 tsp tartare sauce
> 15 ml/1 tbsp tomato purée
> 5 ml/1 tsp Worcestershire sauce
> A few drops of tabasco sauce

Method

1. Mix together all the ingredients well and chill.

2. Serve with seafood dishes.

Serves 4

8 Yoghurt Sauce

Ingredients

> 250 ml/8 fl oz/1 cup Greek yoghurt
> 3 cloves garlic, crushed
> 30 ml/2 tbsp olive oil
> Salt and freshly ground black pepper

Method

1. Place a layer of muslin or thick kitchen paper in a sieve and add the yoghurt. Leave to drain for 30 minutes.

2. Mix the garlic and olive oil thoroughly into the yoghurt and season well with salt and pepper. Chill thoroughly.

3. Serve with seafood or raw vegetables.

Serves 4

Index